M000313224

The Alien's Guidebook Series

The Fiction Writer
Get Published, Write Now!

The ABC's of Good Writing,
One Letter at a Time

By

Nina Munteanu

Starfire World Syndicate

The Fiction Writer: Get Published, Write Now!

Cover Design and Typography: Virginia O'Dine
Interior Design and Illustrations: Nina Munteanu
Graphics for Starfire World Syndicate: David Howton

Cover image is a Galaxy Evolution Explorer observation of the large galaxy in Andromeda, Messier 31.

Published in United States by

Starfire World Syndicate
1039 Everett Avenue, Ste 37
Louisville, 40204, KY, United States
www.thepassionatewriter.com

ISBN 978-0-9823783-0-4 Trade paperback (alk. paper)
ISBN 978-0-9823783-1-1 Hardcover (alk. paper)
ISBN 978-0-9823783-2-8 Digital

Library of Congress Control Number: 2009903756

Includes bibliographical references and index

Printed in the United States of America on acid-free paper

Also printed in the United Kingdom. Published in Canada (under Pixl Press, an Imprint of Starfire World Syndicate)
www.pixlpresscanada.com

Table of Contents

Introduction

Since you picked up this book, there's a good chance that you are a serious writer intent on getting published. That's good because this cool guide provides you with a practical toolkit to get you there.

When submitting your work to editors and agents of both fiction and non-fiction, you typically need to provide three things:

1. a query (see Chapter Q);
2. a synopsis (Chapter O); and,
3. sample chapters (see Chapter B and remaining chapters).

Editors of both fiction and non-fiction look for stunning writing and great story telling (yes, even in non-fiction). They seek originality, genuineness and passion in your writing (see Chapter Z).

If you apply what you've learned in this guide and write from the heart, I guarantee that you will publish.

This guide will help you improve your writing. It does not include things like how to shop for markets or how to market your book, or how to promote your book once it gets published. What it does include, however, is anything to do with the writing side of getting published. So, read, learn and go get published!

A ✿ Alien Architecture: Building From Scenes to Worlds

"My head works in pictures," writes Jon Robertson in an article in Writer's Digest (February, 2008). "Writing projects come to me in pictures too. When I'm writing a book, I keep the job organized in my mind with a metaphor: it's like building a house."

When you're building a house you start with an architectural plan. The plan provides directions for the structural aspects of the house, based on the form decided upon. This is the same for fiction.

Start Building: Structure & Form

"Mention words such as structure, form or plot to some fiction writers," says Jack Bickham, author of *Elements of Writing Fiction: Scene and Structure*, "and they blanch." Bickham suggests that many believe this terminology to be restricttive in the creative process. "Nothing could be further from the truth," says Bickham. "In reality, a thorough understanding and use of fiction's classic structural patterns *frees* the writer from having to worry about the wrong things and allows her to concentrate her imagination on characters and events."

Structure is a process; it "is nothing more than a

way of looking at your story material so that it's organized in a way that's both logical and dramatic," says Bickham. **Structure**, explains Bickham, is the internal part of the story, like the braces or frame of your house; while **form** is external, what you do with the structure—like whether it's a small bungalow or a ten-story office building.

Structure and form are linked; you need to consider both together. For instance, a builder constructing a bungalow wouldn't use the same materials as those for a ten-story office building. On the other hand many of the same principals of construction apply to both projects. "It's the same with fiction," says Bickham. "Story length, author intention, traditional expectations of the audience ...may affect the form a story may take. But underneath most forms lies the same structure—  the same unchanging principles, the same creative laws."

Bickham tells us that most modern fiction relies on the structure of the scene in a larger architectural plan; a series of scenes and bridge sequels that carry the plot of the modern fiction story (see Chapter P). This series of scenes "interconnect in a very clear way to form a long narrative with linear development from the posing of the story question at the outset to the answering of that question at the climax."

Scenes to Worlds

Most writers will tell you that the scene, not the sentence or word, is the smallest component—the building block—of a story. The scene forms an integral part of a larger plot structure that consists of a series of dual scenes and sequels. Dwight Swain, author of *Techniques of the Selling Writer*, breaks these down further into:

- **Scene**: goal, conflict, disaster
- **Sequel**: reaction, dilemma, decision

In Chapter P, I go into some detail describing these stages in plot structure.

Steps in Building Your "House"

Jon Robertson provides these basic steps in a writing project:

Blueprint: it's good to start with an architectural plan or outline. Not everyone writes to an outline, but it's certainly easier if you do. And, contrary to what some might tell you, an outline doesn't mean you can't be spontaneous and intuitive in your writing. It just means that you are more in tune with where your story is going, which makes it more efficient. This is particularly important when working to a deadline.

Excavation and Foundation: how many times have you heard it: location, location, location! The research you conduct on your novel should help you take theme and plotline where they should go. This includes casting your setting,

7

time period and circumstance with your characters. Does it make sense, for instance, to have a character you've given a twenty-first-century city-like demeanor represent someone from the eighteenth-century countryside?

Framing: define your characters' roles and integrate plotlines to create a multilayered storyline. Check your research against storyline, character motivation, plot arguments, etc. This might be where you decide to merge a few characters with redundant roles, or get rid of an entire subplot to add clarity to the main story.

Plumbing, Heating & Electricity: flesh out minor characters according to their roles in the plot; add details to setting. Just as you need to ensure these elements are to code by an inspection, it is wise to review the facts of your book and the logical plot elements that you researched so carefully during the foundation-laying stage of the story.

Wallboard: rewrites and edits help to create the impeccable language that "hides" the work done to create a seamless story. At this stage in writing, paragraphs, sentences and words are inspected for flow, cadence, and tone. Sensual language is increased. Look to heighten smells, sounds, and textures in your protagonist's experiences.

Plaster and Paint: as with wallboard, this is the "polish" that professional writers and editors talk about; passing through the house a few times, like an inspector. This is when you pay attention to the use of literary techniques to create the very best prose you can; check for spelling and grammar, use of active vs. passive verbs, overuse of modifiers. Reading out loud can help.

Building to Code

Below, I summarize Jon Robertson's "building codes" for writing a story that will stand up to the weathers of criticism and readers' expectations:

1. Know your maximum allowable space: know the scope of your story.
2. For a solid foundation, look at your premise in several ways to make sure you understand causality and roles of each character and scene.
3. Use keywords to keep you on track with the design: (e.g., what's it about? Some writers I know keep this above their computer to remind them where their story must lead).
4. Get rid of the clutter to achieve a clean design; at this stage you can still move sections around to achieve the story promise in the beginning. You may even remove a character who has become redundant by merging two characters who serve the same plot device.
5. Frame your story according to your outline; revisit your beginning and ending to ensure you are taking the reader where you intend.
6. "Hide the wiring and plumbing of your surprises, discoveries and revelations behind the walls of your prose." Work on metaphor, word devices, strengthening

9

your word choices, use of powerful verbs.

7. In later drafts, refine color, texture, mood and word choice with careful revision.

8. Finish off your creation by polishing words, sentences, paragraphs, etc. through yet one more revision process.

The Difference Between "Setting" & "World"

Building a "set" or "setting" is one thing; building a "world" is quite another.

In Chapter H, I describe the importance and use of "setting" in story. The setting of a story provides its tone and feel. The place and circumstance in which you place your story help to define its emotional quality.

When setting your story (e.g., location, time, season, weather), you recreate what is already there, but give it a unique quality specific to your story. You characterize it with eccentricities and other qualities that make it memorable and relevant to the story plot and characters. You create "atmosphere." Kimberly Appelcline, creative writing instructor at San Francisco State University, describes atmosphere as "the overall 'feeling' to a place: romantic, threatening, welcoming" which depends largely on your word choice. For instance, "a room with 'oppressive low ceilings and blood-red curtains' feels much different to a reader than a room with 'cozy low ceilings and cheerful red curtains.' "

When you build an entire world, you create far more than atmosphere; you create a civilization, a political structure, a culture and *zeitgeist* as backdrop and influence to story. Consider these epics and the world the author created:

- Jacqueline Carey's *Kushiel's Dart*
- J.R.R. Tolkien's *Lord of the Rings*
- J.K. Rowling's *Harry Potter* series
- Arthur C. Clarke's *Rendezvous with Rama*
- Philip Pullman's *Dark Materials* trilogy
- Larry Niven's *Ringworld*
- Vernor Vinge's *A Fire Upon the Deep*
- Ursula LeGuin's *Left Hand of Darkness* or *Earthsea* series

Although not all fantasy or science fiction novels involve major world-building many do.

Some writers define world-building as the process of constructing an imaginary world, usually associated with a fictional universe, and sometimes called a *constructed world*, *conworld* or *sub-creation.*

Popularized at science fiction workshops during the 1970s, the term according to Brian Stableford, author of *Historical Dictionary of Science Fiction*, describes the development of an imaginary setting that is coherent and possesses a history, geography and ecology.

Where to Start with World-Building

As I already mentioned, most fantasy and

science fiction stories, particularly stories in the long form, require some world-building.

Fantasy author Patricia C. Wrede provides a list of things to consider when you are world-building. I've summarized them in Table 1.

Table 1: World-Building Categories

Categories	Things to Consider
The World	Basics, alternate Earth, not Earth
Physical and Historical Features	General, climate, geography, natural resources, world and regional history
Magic and Magicians	Rules of magic, wizards, magic and technology
Peoples and Customs	Customs, eating, greeting, gestures, visits, language, ethics, values, religion, God(s), populations
Social Organization	Government, politics, legal system, foreign relations, war and weapons
Commerce, Trade and Public Life	Business and industry, transportation, communication, science & technology, medicine, arts, entertainment, architecture, urban versus rural influences
Daily Life	Fashion, dress, manners, diet, education, calendar

Wrede's article provides lots of relevant and detailed questions for each of these categories. For instance, when considering just the "basics" in your world, Wrede suggests you address

these questions among any others you may
already have:

- Are the laws of nature and physics
  actually different in this world, or are they
  the same as in real life? How does magic
  fit in? How do magical beasts fit in?

- Is this generally an earth-like world? Is it
  an "alternate Earth"?

- Are there different human/other races?
  What is the cultural and ethnic diversity of
  this world?

- How long have there been people on this
  world? Did they evolve, or did they
  migrate from somewhere/when else?

- How many people are there in this
  country? How does this compare with the
  world population? What is considered a
  small town/large town/city?

- Where does magic power come from: the
  gods, the "mana" of the world, the
  personal willpower or life force of the
  magician? Is magic an exhaustible resource? Do different races/species have
  different sources for their magic, or does
  everybody use the same one?

In a world that is not Earth, she asks these
questions:

- How does this world differ physically from
  earth? Is it the same size (same density,
  same gravity), same ratio of land/water,
  same atmosphere, etc.? Does it have

more than one sun or moon? Rings? Are there spectacular constellations/comets, etc. visible at night or by day?

- Are there non-human inhabitants (elves, dwarves, aliens)? If so, how many? How openly present? What areas do they occupy?

- How are the continents laid out? If there is more than one moon/sun, how does this affect winds, tides and weather generally?

- How much land is there, and how much of it is habitable?

- Is the axial tilt and orbit the same—i.e., does the world have the same seasons and same length of year as Earth?

Do You Need Science To Make a Believable World?

The short answer is: it depends on what kind of story you're writing. If it's a historical fantasy set on Earth, no; if it's set on some probable planet in the Andromeda Galaxy, the answer is yes. But, in both cases you owe the reader to be accurate and to do the proper research (see Chapter W).

Part of the reason people read historical epics is to learn more about that particular civilization and time period. Your reader trusts that you will give her the facts on the world, while taking liberties on the remaining story elements. Similarly, a science fiction reader opens the first book in

Larry Niven's *Ringworld* series with the expectation of learning about a made-up world based on principles of science.

When doing your research for building another world, the science can get a little tricky, if not downright intimidating. My background is in ecology (the science of environments), so I come by this rather easily, but if your background isn't in science, should you even attempt it? Don't despair. And read on.

A lot of science fiction is written by nonscientists. That said, many science fiction readers—particularly those who enjoy hard science fiction—expect your science to be not only plausible but somewhat proven and your premise to be based upon sound scientific principle. They expect your research to be impeccable because they are expecting to learn something—in science.

Nebula and Hugo Award-winning SF author Robert J. Sawyer gives two pieces of advice:

1. "Read the magazines *Discover, New Scientist, Science News,* and *Scientific American.*" These are excellent sources of up-to-date news in the science field that are written in accessible language. [For the latest in cool science topics written to be understood by anyone, read my blog *The Alien Next Door.*]

15

2. "The only way to write SF successfully is to read it. An excellent *SF 101* course would be to read all the Hugo and Nebula-winning novels, as well as the annual reprint anthologies *The Year's Best Science Fiction* edited by Gardner Dozois (St. Martin's) and *Year's Best SF* edited by David G. Hartwell and Kathryn Cramer (Eos)."

What's important to remember is that the world you build is part of the story. It isn't just a lot of "interesting" detail. As I mention in Chapter H for "setting", the world you build, like a character in your story, plays a role in defining and supporting its theme. The major qualities of your world are, therefore, best derived for plot and thematic reasons—which come from "story". The rest—the details—are things you can find in books or websites, or get from experts in your local university, etc. Don't let science intimidate you but ensure that you get it right by using your resources and verifying your information with an expert. Use your local libraries, universities, colleges, and online resources. Interview scientists, technical people and other writers. That's part of being a writer too (see Chapter I).

World-Builder's Disease?

"Fantasy writers have a penchant for working up histories of imaginary empires that can run for hundreds of pages, full of maps and chronologies and genealogical trees a yard long," says Ansen Dibell, author of *The Elements of Writing Fiction: Plot.* "Similarly, science fiction writers can fall in love with their hardware and want to

16

show it off," he adds and describes this as a kind of narrative cancer, a "World-Builder's disease."

I've seen evidence of both. I must confess to a favorite practice of keeping a scrapbook of detailed background material on each of my projects and universes that I've constructed (see Chapter W for details). These books are rich in their own right with factual and, at times, diverting information about my created world. Most of us who world-build keep extensive files of background information on our worlds. In some cases, these can be published as companions to the main book series (e.g., J.K. Rowling's books on Quiddich or magical creatures, which most certainly came from her extensive background notes). Dibell's point is that this information doesn't belong in the main book, where it can interfere with the process of storytelling. It becomes "info dump", which, as I explain in Chapter E, is often very static, lacks drama, and proves ultimately boring.

References

Appelcline, Kimberly. 2008. "Writing Dynamic Settings". In: *Skotos Articles.*
http://www.skotos.net/articles/DynamicSettings.html

Bickham, Jack. 1993. *Elements of Fiction Writing: Scene and Structure.* Writer's Digest Books. Cincinnati, Ohio.

Dibell, Ansen. 1988. *Elements of Fiction Writing: Plot.* Writer's Digest Books. Cincinnati, Ohio.

Gillet, Stephen. 2001. *World Building (Science Fiction Writing).* Writer's Digest Books. Cincinnati, Ohio. 198pp.

Robertson, Jon. 2008. "Write from the Ground Up". In: *Writer's Digest.* February, 2008.

Sawyer, Robert J. 2008. "Eight Things Science Fiction

17

Writers Need To Know." In: The Intimately Human & The Grandly Cosmic Master Class, Surrey International Writers' Conference 2008, October 24-26. Surrey, British Columbia.

Stableford, Brian M. 2004. *Historical Dictionary of Science Fiction.* Scarecrow Press.

Swain, Dwight. 1982. *Techniques of the Selling Writer.* University of Oklahoma Press. 330pp.

Wrede, Patricia C. 2005. "Fantasy World Building Questions" In: SFWA.
http://www.sfwa.org/writing/worldbuilding1.htm

B. ❤ Blazing Beginnings

First sentences are doors to worlds
—Ursula Le Guin

"A novel is like a car," says Sol Stein (*Sol Stein on Writing*). "It won't go anywhere until you start the engine." It's when the engine is running that the reader decides not to put the book down. The opening of a story should be in motion. It should sweep the reader into the story. It doesn't need to be wild action. It just needs to compel the reader to want to know more. This is accomplished by engaging the reader with "intrigue". Author Jane Eaton Hamilton suggested several options. These include: introduce conflict; threaten a likeable character; reveal an unusual character or situation.

Arouse, Delay and Reward...

In an April 2001 article of *Writer's Digest*, Joe Cardillo (director of Southern Vermont College's creative writing program) suggested that the three elements of hooking a reader resemble the steps he uses to train his Samoyed puppy: 1) arouse interest; 2) delay, then 3) reward.

The writer arouses interest in the reader by providing enough detail to get the reader to ask questions. Now they want something. You tease them with the delay; that keeps them reading and turning the pages. It also gives them the chance to try to come up with the answers themselves. In some books it can be a game between reader and writer; can the reader come up with the answer before the writer provides it? The reward comes in stages. Don't answer all the questions at once. Parcel them out slowly. That's what the book—the story—is for.

In his New York Times bestselling book, *The Golden Compass*, Philip Pullman begins with a rich, though judicious, description of a meeting room in the university where our protagonist is slinking with her companion, Pantalaimon. The reader is intrigued; what important function is about to happen? Then Pullman steps up the intrigue:

> Lyra stopped by the Master's chair and flicked the biggest glass gently with a fingernail. The sound rang clearly through the hall.
> "You're not taking this seriously," whispered her daemon. "Behave yourself."
> "They're making too much noise to hear from the kitchen," Lyra whispered back. "And the steward doesn't come in till the first bell. Stop fussing."
> But she put her palm over the ringing crystal anyway, and Panalaimon fluttered ahead and through the slightly open door of the Retiring Room at the other end of the dais. After a moment he appeared again.
> "There's no one there," he whispered. "But we must be quick."

Now we are really intrigued. And we have some major questions that need answering. What are these two doing there and what will happen to them? But Pullman delays by continuing to provide rich background, all important to the setting of the scene. And, through actions by Lyra and Pantalaimon, Pullman gives us information about these already intriguing and endearing characters:

> She sat in one of the green leather armchairs. It was so deep she found herself nearly lying down, but she sat up again and tucked her legs under her to look at the portraits on the wall. More old Scholars, probably; robed, bearded, and gloomy, they stared out of their frames in solemn disapproval.
> "What d'you think they talk about?" Lyra said, or began to say, because before she'd finished the question she heard voices outside the door.
> "Behind the chair—quick!" whispered Pantalaimon, and in a flash Lyra was out of the armchair and crouching behind it. It wasn't the best one for hiding behind: she'd chosen one in the very center of the room, and unless she kept very quiet...

Now we begin to get some answers and in the most delicious way: as accomplices in hiding, with the risk of being found. However, Pullman provides the "reward" in very small doses and over many pages, luring the reader deeper and deeper into the novel. And, by the way, in case you were curious, she *does* get caught!

Opening as Story Promise

There is no beginning without an end. In a workshop at the 1998 Surrey Writer's Conference Elizabeth Lyon, author of *The Sell Your Novel Tool Kit* (2002), suggested that the beginning of a novel should "reflect the entire book. There should be a tie-in [between] the beginning and the end." This is sometimes called "framing" a story, where the principal thematic problem is given in the beginning and then resolved in the end.

 Bill Johnson, author of *A Story is a Promise*, describes it as a promise to the reader. The beginning of a book sets up a covenant between writer and reader, a covenant for a journey they will take together toward resolution. Johnson describes the story promise as doing three things, similar to Cardillo's three steps (arouse, delay, reward). Johnson calls them setting out a story's core dramatic issue (the promise), movement, and fulfillment of the promise.

"Dramatic story-issues revolve around issues of human need. The need to be loved. To have control of one's fate. To feel a sense of purpose. To be able to overcome obstacles. To be able to grow and heal from life's wounds. To understand and make sense of the events of life." He warns that "if you can't name the issue at the heart of your story, it risks being unclear to your audience."

Regarding movement, Johnson says, "To understand the general movement of a story— fear to courage, hate to love, ignorance to understanding—enables a storyteller to better understand what types of characters, events, and environments serve the dramatic purpose of a particular story."

Fulfillment, of course, occurs for both reader and the story's character when he or she gains or achieves resolution of the story's promise. It is important for the writer to understand that this pattern is something that is repeatedly used from every scene to the entire novel (see Chapter J).

"One tendency of apprentice writers," says Rachel Simon, author of *Riding the Bus with my Sister*, "is to begin in a way that is boring. The two most common boring openings are a character waking up in bed, and a character traveling to where the rest of the story occurs. These are so overused and tedious that editors and many readers are likely to read no further." Elizabeth Lyon adds these two cliché openings to avoid: a character dreaming; or standing in front of a mirror to describe him/herself.

"Start your book with a scene where something is happening, and action takes place; show the drama not the reaction to it," says Lyon. In other words, start near the climax of the scene, in mid-action. She warns that "too much narrative—also

23

flashback and exposition—[kill the first chapter]." She suggests that you "first get the character moving forward. Get into the plot. Don't get into indigestible chunks of narration. After the first major crisis, you can give more background information. Avoid revealing everything at once; reveal slowly, like pieces of a puzzle." Beginning writers all too often succumb to the urge to over-describe character, set-ting, and situation. This is usually due to inex-perience and lack of confidence in your reader.

Openings Agents Hate

In an article for Writer's Digest (October 2008) Chuck Sambuchino, edi-tor of *Guide to Literary Agents*, interviewed several agents about what kind of openings peeved them. Their responses were classic and I include a few choice ones here as examples of what NOT to do:

> "Most agents hate prologues. Just make the first chapter relevant and well written."—Andrea Brown, Andrea Brown Literary Agency

> "Slow writing with a lot of description puts me off very quickly. I like a first chapter that moves quickly and draws me in so I'm immediately hooked."—Andrea Hurst, Andrea Hurst Literary Management

"I hate it when a book begins with an adventure that turns out to be a dream at the end of the chapter."—Mollie Glick, Jean V. Naggar Literary Agency

"I [dislike] inauthentic dialogue to tell the reader who the characters are, instead of showing who the characters are."—Jennifer Cayea, *Avenue A Literary*

"I'm turned off when a writer feels the need to fill in all the back story before starting the story; a story that opens on the protagonist's mental reflection of their situation is a red flag."—Stephany Evans, *FinePrint Literary Management*

"One of the biggest problems is the 'information dump' in the first few pages, where the author is trying to tell us everything we supposedly need to know to understand the story. Getting to know characters in a story is like getting to know people in real life. You find out their personality and details of their life over time."—Rachelle Gardner, *WordServe Literary*

I want you to pay specific attention to the last remark by Rachelle Gardner. This is a very common symptom of beginners. And a logical one. As beginners, we have not yet gained the confidence that comes with experience to trust that we won't lose the reader if we don't tell them everything right away. The key is to choose just enough to whet their appetite for more. And, yes, it is critical what you choose.

To help you choose which details to reveal at the very beginning, think of yourself as a poet, having to be spare about the words you choose. Remember Elizabeth Lyon's advice of addressing the main theme that will be revisited in the end. Think of that frame.

Last Words—Titles

In fact, the words of the title of your story are the very first a reader will encounter of your work.

Maya Kaathryn Bohnhoff, author of *The Crystal Rose*, asserts that "titles can determine whether a story is read, in what spirit it's read, and whether it's remembered by name or forgotten. They can be like store windows that offer a tantalizing glimpse of what's inside, or they can give away the entire inventory."

The best titles are those that grow naturally out of the subject matter and capture the emotion and heart of the story. They can be a play on words, convey several meanings, be a metaphor or a contradiction or irony. Think of the titles of some of your favorite books; how do they convey the core of the story without giving it away? Think of these titles and what they convey, and don't give away: *Gone With the Wind. White Oleander. The Golden Compass. The Return of the Native. Doctor Zhivago. A Tale of Two Cities. The Prisoner of Azkaban. Lady Chatterley's*

Lover. The Iliad. Pale Fire. Lord of the Flies, Calculating God.

I chose the title, *Collision with Paradise* for my science fiction romantic thriller to convey the paradox of conflict and action (in collision) with the quest for well-being (paradise) that reflected my lead character's own conflict. The two juxtaposed as oxymoron made the title provocative and readers became naturally curious. My science fiction novel, *Darwin's Paradox*, used this term on several levels to convey a complex story about the paradox of evolution.

Exercise:

1. Pick up several books you admire and read their opening sentences. Compare and contrast each specific opening (and its related overall story) to the others. How does each show that a change is imminent? What is the story promise?

2. Pick ten random titles of books from your bookshelf and analyze how the opening conveys the story. Do they work? If so, why? If not, why not?

References

Bohnhoff, Maya Kaathryn. 1999. "Taming the Fictional Wilds". In: *Fiction Writer*. April. 1999.

Cardillo, Joe. 2001. "Three Ways to Keep Your Readers Hooked". *Writer's Digest*, April, 2001, volume 81, no. 4.

Johnson, Bill. 2000. *A Story Is a Promise*. Blue Heron Publishing. Portland, Oregon. 187pp.

Lyon, Elizabeth. 2002. *The Sell Your Novel Took Kit*. Revised Edition. Perigee Trade. 320pp.

Pullman, Philip. *The Golden Compass*. Del Ray, New York. 351pp.

Sambuchino, Chuck. 2008. "What Agents Hate". *Writer's Digest*, October, 2008, volume 88, no. 5.

Stein, Sol. 2000. *Stein on Writing*. St. Martin's Griffin, New York. 308pp.

C ❤ Charismatic Characters

"Characters in your book are people," says Orson Scott Card in *Elements of Writing Fiction: Characters & Viewpoint.* "Yes, I know you made them up," he continues, "but readers want your characters to seem like real people...readers want to get to know your characters as well as they know their own friends, their own family. As well as they know themselves. No—better than they know any living person."

What is a Character?

To begin with, *a character is what she does*, says Orson Scott Card. He gives the example of Indiana Jones in the introductory scene of *Raiders of the Lost Ark*, in which we see through action what kind of man he is: "within ten minutes of the beginning of the movie, we knew that Indiana Jones was resourceful, greedy, clever, brave, intense, that he didn't take himself too seriously; that he was determined to survive against all odds." But this is just the beginning of describing a character. Characters can be further described through "stereotype," "motive," "habits and patterns," "talents and abilities," "tastes and preferences," "body" and through knowing something of their "past" or "reputation" suggests Scott Card. "Part of a character's identity is what others say about him," says Scott Card.

The Character's Role

Your characters have a dramatic function, a role in advancing the plot and/or theme; they need a reason to be there. Your characters are the most important part of your book (more so than the plot or premise). Through them your book lives and breathes. Through them your premise, idea and your plot come alive. Through them you achieve empathy and commitment from the reader and a willingness to keep reading to find out what's going to happen next: if the reader doesn't invest in the characters, she won't really care what happens next.

Dramatic function aside, in order for your character to be memorable he needs to have a charismatic personality. He needs to show qualities that make him distinctive.

All memorable characters show some character development (as story arc) from beginning to end of story. The more your character changes over a story, the more he will be noticed.

Good Fictional Characters

Characters need to "appear" real without "being" real. For instance, in real life a person may act through no apparent motivation, be confusing, incoherent, etc. Characters in fiction fulfill a dramatic function in the story for the reader and are, therefore, more logically laid out. They may, as a result, be more coherent, consistent and clear in their actions and qualities than a person in real life.

Fictional characters come to life by giving them individual traits, real weaknesses and heroic qualities that readers can recognize and empathize with. You play these against each other to achieve drama. For instance, a man who is afraid of heights but who must climb a mountain to save his love is far more compelling than one who is not; a military man who fears responsibility but must lead his team into battle; a shy scientist impelled to discovery; etc.

Characters written by beginning writers often suffer from lack of distinction, or purpose, and just clutter up a story. For a character to "come alive" their "voice" must be unique (see Chapter V). Give them distinctive body movements,  dress, facial features and expressions that reveal inner feelings, emotions, fears, motivations, etc. Then keep them consistent. Writers use several techniques to achieve distinctiveness and increase empathy for a character, including:

- use of first person or third person point of view (POV)
- focusing on fewer rather than many characters
- creating character dossiers and keeping them consistent
- providing each character with a distinctive "voice" (figuratively), as in how they behave and react, what they say etc.

Use of vernacular distinguishes character and how they relate to their setting (see Chapter H)

Make your characters argue or disagree (at least!) over what they believe in—or don't believe in. Give them suspicions, have them betray and ridicule one another. This increases tension and conflict (two things every book requires) and enlightens the reader on plot and theme. Describe your characters vividly as the reader encounters them.

In his book, *Characters & Viewpoint*, Orson Scott Card suggests that when a reader begins your story, he may ask three challenging questions, which if not sufficiently answered, may drive him to put the book down:

- *"So what?"* Why should I care about what's going on?

- *"Oh, yeah?"* Come on. I don't believe anyone would do that.

- *"Huh?"* What's happening? This doesn't make any sense. I don't get it.

It helps if the writer asks causal questions like: *what made this happen? Why did it happen and what was its effect?* Orson Scott Card mentions questions that open up story and character possibilities, such as: *what can go wrong? Who*

32

would suffer the most?

Here are some more questions you need to ask about your characters:

1. If you can remove the character, will the book fall apart? (If not, you don't need that character; they aren't fulfilling a role in the book)
2. How does the character portray the major or minor theme of the book? That's what characters are there for
3. What is the role of the character? (E.g., protagonist, antagonist, mentor, catalyst, etc.)
4. What is the story arc of the character? Does s/he develop or change, learn something by the end? If not, s/he will be two-dimensional and less interesting
5. What major obstacle(s) must your character overcome?
6. Who are your major protagonist(s)—the main character who changes the most?
7. Who are your major antagonist(s)—those who provide the most trouble for your protagonists, the source of conflict and tension?
8. What's at stake: for the world (plot); for each individual (theme) and how do these tie together?

To summarize, each character is there for a purpose and this needs to be made apparent to the reader (intuitively, through characterization, their failings, weaknesses, etc.). Orson Scott Card reminds us that "real people are who they are—you love 'em or leave 'em. But fictional characters have a job to do."

Make your character bleed, hurt, cry, and feel. This needs to be clear to the reader, who wants to empathize with some of them and hate others. How characters interact with their surroundings and each other creates tension, a key element to good storytelling.

Tension, of course, builds further with the additional conflict of protagonist with antagonists. In  truth, it's more fun to read about the tension from WITHIN a group that's supposed to be together. Think of Harry Potter and what was juicy there. It wasn't Voldemort that made the story so memorable for me and didn't let me put down the book until I'd finished it so much as what went on at Hogwarts between Harry and his friends and not-so-friends.

Types of Characters & Archetypes

In keeping with their dramatic function in the story, characters may be categorized in many ways, aside from protagonist (central figure of the story) and antagonist (main opponent of the protagonist) or main character versus minor character. While these are valid designations, they do not generally describe the type of character in question. The type of character may vary greatly but can generally fit into one of several archetypes.

In psychology, an **archetype** is a model of a person, personality or behavior. For instance, a mother figure is an archetype. Archetypes are found in nearly all forms of literature, with their motifs being mostly rooted in folklore. Archetypes are openly used in allegories and ancient myth/poems. They are easily recognized by their clearly allegorical concepts and names: for instance, Red Crosse, the Christian knight in Edmund Spenser's epic poem, *The Faerie Queen*, represents the virtue of holiness and ultimately all Christian souls in search of truth.

Chris Vogler, author of *The Writer's Journey: Mythic Structure for Writers*, describes six major archetypes that the main character or hero archetype may encounter during her story arc (see Chapter J). These include: mentor, herald, threshold guardian, trickster, shape shifter and shadow.

Carol S. Pearson provides further categories for hero-archetypes, including: innocent, orphan, martyr, wanderer, warrior, caregiver, seeker, lover, destroyer, creator, ruler, magician, sage, and fool.

Character & Premise

Robert J. Sawyer reminds us that "story-people are made-to-order to do a specific job." This notion goes back "twenty-five hundred years to the classical playwrights," says Sawyer. "In Greek tragedy, the main character was always specifically designed to fit the particular plot.

Indeed, each protagonist was constructed with an intrinsic *hamartia*, or tragic flaw, keyed directly to the story's theme."

Among several examples, Sawyer cites Frederick Pohl's *Gateway*, whose premise was that near a black hole, the passage of time slows to a stop. Pohl's character, Robinette Broadhead, had done something horrible to people he'd left behind, near a black hole. "The story is told through psychoanalytic sessions," says Sawyer. "Robinette can't get over his guilt because no matter how many years pass for him, it's always that one terrible moment of betrayal for those he's left behind. The novel works spectacularly."

"The lesson is simple," says Sawyer: "your main character should illuminate the fundamental conflict suggested by your premise."

What this translates to is that for you to start with a character then go looking for a story will be more challenging than the other way around. It is easier to fit a character to a premise to best serve a dramatic function. For instance, Sawyer's example of a premise is: you want to write about a "telepathic alien who can read subconscious instead of conscious thoughts." You then need to come up with a character who would best dramatize the issues in the premise: for instance, a man who's been suppressing terrible memories of the suicide of his wife.

Sawyer was thinking of a story already written: *Solaris* by Stanislaw Lem.

Too Many Characters?

One manuscript I critiqued for a student, contained a dizzying cast of characters ranging from men and women on various quests to elves, dragons, witches and several made up creatures. "A large cast *can* be used successfully, says Maya Kaathryn Bohnhoff, author of *The Crystal Rose*, "but only if each character is given a clearly distinguishable personality and role."

Each character provides a **function** and possesses an emotional and narrative **weight**. Together, function and weight achieve a **balance**. For instance, explains Bohnhoff, a character who serves as a foil should balance the protagonist with an equal weight. Otherwise the reader won't believe the match-up and it won't work.

Exercise:

3. Pick five books at random and describe the main character. What distinguishes him/her? Create a dossier on him/her; include a list of their faults (weaknesses) and their heroic qualities (strengths). Now, pick that character's foil and do the same. How do they match?

4. Describe the premise of a story you are writing (see Chapters B and O for ideas) then match it with your main characters. How do their traits dramatize the premise? What changes or additions could you make to your characters to better dramatize your premise?

References

Bohnhoff, Maya Kaathryn. 1999. "Taming the Fictional Wilds". In: *Fiction Writer*. April, 1999.

Pearson, Carol S. 1998. *The Hero Within: Six Archetypes We Live By*. Harper. San Francisco. 3rd Edition.

Scott Card, Orson. 1999. *Elements of Writing Fiction: Characters & Viewpoint*. Writer's Digest Books. 182pp.

Sawyer, Robert. J. 1995. "On Writing: Constructing Characters." In: *SF Writer*. http://www.sfwriter.com/ow02.htm

Vogler, Christopher. 1998. *The Writer's Journey: Mythic Structure for Writers*. 2nd Edition. Michael Wiese Productions, Studio City, California. 326pp.

D. ● Get the Dope on Dialogue...He said, She said!

One of the most important devices to spice up narrative and increase pace is the use of dialogue. There's a reason for this: we read dialogue more quickly; it's written in more fluid, conversational English; it tends to create more white space on a page with less dense text, more pleasing to the reader's eye. Dialogue is action. It gets readers involved.

What Dialogue Is and What Dialogue Isn't

Good dialogue neither mimics actual speech (i.e., it's not usually mundane, repetitive or broken with words like "uh") nor does it educate the reader through long discourse (unless the character is that kind of person). Good dialogue in a story should be somewhere in the middle. While it should read as fluid conversation, dialogue remains a device to propel the plot or enlighten us to the character of the speaker. No conversation follows a perfect linear progression. People interrupt one another, talk over one another, often don't answer questions posed to them or avoid them by not answering them directly. These can all be used by the writer to establish character, tension, and relationship.

Jane Eaton Hamilton, author of *Hunger*, suggests that good dialogue does one or several of the following:

- Moves the story along
- Describes a character
- Describes setting
- Describes an object
- Crystallizes relationships and situations
- Allows characters to confront each other (conflict is essential in a story)
- Delivers a punch or deciding blow in a conflict
- Offers a cue for transition to a new scene
- Increases tension
- Speeds up pace

Tips for Good Dialogue

Below, I provide a few tips when using dialogue in your story.

- **Show, don't tell**: a common error of beginning writers is to use dialogue to explain something that both participants should already know but the reader doesn't. It is both awkward and unrealistic and immediately exposes you as a novice. For instance, avoid the use of "As you know..." It's better to keep the reader in the dark for a while than to use dialogue to explain something.

- **Have your characters talk to each other, not to the reader**: for instance, "Hello, John, you loser drunk and wayward son of the most feared gangster in town!" could be improved to, "You stink like a distillery, John! Wait 'til papa's thugs find you!"

- **Avoid adverbs**: e.g., he said *dramatically*, she said *pleadingly*; instead look for better ways to express the way they said it with actual dialogue. That's not to say you can't use adverbs (I believe J.K. Rowling is notorious for this), just use them sparingly and judiciously.

- **Avoid tag lines that repeat what the dialogue already tells the reader**: e.g., "I'm sorry," he *apologized*. "Can I help you?" she *asked*.

- **Avoid over-explaining**: e.g., "He can't be there!" she said in disbelief. *Disbelief* is redundant to the dialogue.

- **Use interrupted speech**: people cut each other off or talk over one another all the time. This can be incorporated into your dialogue as well, to achieve that note of hastiness, rudeness, abruptness, etc.

- **He said, she said**: reduce tag lines where possible and keep them simple by using "said"; another sign of a novice is the overuse of words other than said (e.g., snarled, hissed, purred, etc.). While these can add spice, keep them for special places as

41

they are noticed by the reader and will distract otherwise. In fact, the use of he said, she said is recommended throughout. Think of them as punctuation. Avoid long dialogue without a tag—your reader needs to know who said what.

- **Pay consistent attention to a character's "voice"**: each character has a way of speaking that identifies them as a certain type of person. This can be used to identify class, education, culture, ethnicity, proclivities, etc. For instance one character might use Oxford English and another might swear every third word.

- **Use speech signatures**: pick out particular word phrases for characters that can be their own and can be identified with them. If they have additional metaphoric meaning to the story, even better. For instance, I know a person who always adds "Don't you think?" to almost everything he says. This says something about how that person… well, thinks… I knew another person who always added "Do you see?" at the end of his phrase. Again rather revealing.

- **Intersperse dialogue with good descriptive narrative**: don't forget to keep the reader plugged into the setting. Many

42

beginning writers forget to "ground" the reader with sufficient cues as to where the characters are and what they're doing while they are having this great conversation. This phenomenon is so common, it even has a name. It's called "talking heads."

- **Use indirect conversation with oblique answers or overlapping speech**: people often don't respond directly to a question posed them. For instance:

  "Are you calling me from home?"
  "The traffic is crazy! I saw two accidents in the space of one hour."
  "Can you pull out the frozen pizza for dinner?"
  "I hate frozen pizza!"

- **Contradict dialogue with narrative**: when dialogue contradicts body language or other narrative cues about the speaker, this adds an element of tension and heightens the readers' excitement while telling them something important. Here are a few examples:

  "How'd it go?"
  "Great," he lied.

  "I feel so much better now," she said, jaw clenched.
  "It's okay; I believe you." His heart slammed.

43

Well, you get the picture, anyway (ah, I just revealed that I'm a visual thinker)!

Dialogue or Body Language

Because body language is such an interesting device for a writer, let's look at it more closely. It starts with acknowledging and observing body language in others and in yourself.  Kinesics is the study of body language and its intent is to explain how our movements and gestures project a person's hidden thoughts. Blushing is an obvious reaction. But more subtle ones can be used. When body language contradicts verbal expression, the opportunity for tension, conflict and interesting scenarios increases tremendously.

According to Janet Lee Carey, author of *Dragon's Keep*, body language:

- Shows the subtle undercurrent of communications between characters (of which either may not be consciously aware)
- Shows the comic or tragic elements behind the dialogue
- Reveals the character's true feelings (regardless of what he or she is saying).

In order to accomplish this task, the writer must

learn to accurately interpret the subtle signals of other people's body language and translate them into the written form. One way is to look at yourself. Ask yourself: what do you do when you're nervous? Excited? Thrilled? Sad? Angry? How do you do housework when you're angry? When you're happy? It helps to look at the same action under different moods to distill out the finer nuances of gesture and movement. I talk more about this in Chapter T.

Amplification & Contradiction: Subtext

Depending on the interaction between two characters, body language can either amplify verbal expression or contradict it. The latter, of course, is usually more interesting, because it sets up tension and underlying conflict.

The following is an example of **amplification**:

> "So, what happened?" Jenny asked, leaning forward and gazing directly at Mark.

Jenny's body language matches her dialogue, amplifying her genuine concern. Here's an example of **contradiction**:

> "Hey, great to see you," Dave said, crossing his arms and edging back to slouch against the wall.
> Tom wandered to the fridge and opened it to look inside. "Can I have a beer?"
> Dave fixed a hard smile at Tom. "Sure."

It's obvious that Dave isn't happy to see Tom, and his body language contradicts his verbal expression. This makes for compelling reading. Subtext (beneath the surface of dialogue) adds interest and intrigue, particularly when it contradicts or complicates the overt message.

Exercise:

1. Go on a bus ride or some other mass transit, listen to conversation and take notes. Pay attention to vernacular, structure, tone and flow of conversation, body language.

2. Pick a few friends (preferably showing a range of temperament and lifestyle) and ask them the same question. Record and interpret.

3. Write a dialogue in which one of the characters has a secret that you don't reveal to the reader but allow them to figure it out (e.g. between a women who has just lost her job and her husband who has just come home from a tryst with his lover).

References

Carey, Janet Lee. 2007. *Dragon's Keep*. Harcourt. 320pp.

Easton Hamilton, Jane. 2002. *Hunger*. Oberon Press.

E ❂ Exposition & Endless Endings...

What Is Exposition?

According to Arnetha F. Ball, Professor of Education at Stanford University, "Exposition is a type of oral or written discourse that is used to explain, describe, give information or inform."

In fiction, exposition breaks away from the ongoing action of a scene to give information. It can be one paragraph or go on for several pages. Exposition often provides contextual information critical for the reader to buy in to character-motivation or the ideas promoted in the story. It gives a story its perspective and larger meaning by linking the reader with the thematic elements. If scene is action and plot, exposition feeds reflection and theme. Exposition can appear in the form of background, setting, back story or overview. It is most often expressed through a POV character's reflection and observation.

Exposition is something every writer grapples with in a story. Where to put it? When to add it? How much is too much? How little is too little? Working out when to explain the plot and when to leave the reader to draw their own conclusions can be tricky for even experienced writers, says author Elsa Neal. Ansen Dibell, author of *Elements of Fiction Writing: Plot*, describes exposition as "the author telling the reader something—*telling*, rather than *showing*." Telling is much less effective and interesting than showing (see Chapter T). It follows then that exposition is much less dramatic and less vivid than a scene. This is why you need to break exposition up into small bite-size pieces rather than a huge caloric meal of information. A good rule to follow is to minimize exposition as much as you can. This doesn't mean that you need to emulate Hemingway exactly.

In fact, "in science fiction, and medical and forensic fiction," adds Neal, "detailed explanations of processes and their relevance to the plot is expected as part of the genre."

Why Should I Explain?

There are points in almost every story where exposition is necessary. Most stories would suffer without information that adds past, context and overview. "Well-handled exposition gives perspective, dimension and context that help events in the foreground make sense," says Dibell.

Exposition lets you:

- Describe a person in detail

48

- Describe a place for more than a phrase or two (important especially if a place serves as a character—see Chapter H)
- Skip over periods of time when nothing important or compelling is happening, without a jarring break in the narrative
- Draw back from a close-focus action scene to give the reader a meaningful overview (and to say how things got that way)
- Give some background and history of characters, location, event, etc.

Ultimately, by its very nature, exposition also provides a change in pace and a lilting cadence in your story. It's like taking in a sighing breath after a good run. "In practice, fiction is a balance between scene and explanation—70%/30%," says Dibell.

To Expose or Not to Expose...That is the Question...

Okay, it's good to add exposition. But there is a way and a time to do it. You need to balance the show-and-tell part of your narrative and to maintain a rhythm in your pace and tone. This means doing several things:

- **Restrain yourself and keep your notes to yourself:** I've seen excellent writers add too much exposition on a subject that obviously excited them but didn't necessarily excite me. This often occurs when a writer feels impelled to share their invention or discovery at the

49

expense of storytelling. Doing your homework in writing (e.g., research) also includes keeping it to yourself, no matter how much you want to share it. Doing your homework is the iceberg and the story is the tip. Many genre books (e.g., science fiction, thrillers, mysteries, etc.) must be supported by solid research. The writer takes what she needs for the story and keeps the rest. "The iceberg should stay out of sight to anchor the whole, not be on view to weigh it down," Dibell advises.

- **Arouse then explain:** introduce your character by letting her act and show herself and engage the reader's curiosity and sympathy, then explain how and why she got there.

- **Build exposition into the scene:** get creative and include expository information as props in a scene. This is a great way to add information seamlessly.

- **Put exposition in between scenes:** instead of interrupting a scene in action, exposition can be used to give the reader a breather from a high paced scene to reflect along with the protagonist on what just happened. This is a more appropriate place to read exposition, when the reader has calmed down.

- **Let a character explain:** have your characters provide the information by one questioning and the other replying. There is a danger in this kind of exposition, in that the dialogue can become encumbered by long stretches of explanation. Take care to make this realistic and enjoyable to the reader. If done well, this type of exposition can also reveal things about the characters.

- **Use interior monologue:** use a character's inner reflections to reveal information, which also reveals something of the character herself. Be careful not to turn this into polemic, however.

Elsa Neal recommends that you "keep a balance between giving your readers information that they need and allowing them to work out meanings and nuances for themselves." She adds, "On the other hand, do assume that your readers are intelligent. It can be very irritating to read a story in which the writer constantly states the obvious. Unfortunately, books involving details of cutting edge technology inadvertently run the risk of stating the obvious years down the line." She gives the example of Michael Crichton's 1993 book, *Disclosure*, in which he provided an explanation of what a CD-ROM was; to give the same explanation today would insult the reader's intelligence.

When You Reach the End, STOP!

If you ever saw Peter Seller's movie *The Party*, the first scene is priceless. Sellers plays an actor who is shot in a war scene; he subverts the script by refusing to die. His endless death struggles get so annoying that even the men from his own army turn and shoot him.

51

The last thing you want to do is create an ending or dénouement that struggles in its conclusions. This is ultimately not satisfying for the reader.

According to Dibell, endings come in two basic shapes: 1) circular and 2) linear. In a writing workshop I recently participated in, Patrick Rothfuss, author of *The Name of the Wind*, demonstrated two kinds of endings using his hands: for the first kind he clenched his fists in front of him; for the second kind, he opened his hands airily toward his audience. The kind of ending you choose for your story will depend on the kind of story you are telling: one that rises to a climax or one that returns home.

Ending in a Circle

Beginning and ending connect in a circular story. In such a story, the end and the beginning are much more alike than they are to the middle. This is because the end reflects the promise of the beginning. Framed stories use the same technique, except the beginning and end frames are more like bookends, supporting the story from the outside and made of a visibly different structure (for example in prologue and epilogue), fashion and often in different POV, tense, style, etc.).

Circular endings, and their circular stories, are

often the shape that quest-adventure stories take on (see Chapter J, The Hero's Journey). The main character sets out on a quest to find or learn or accomplish something, passes through trials, and finally succeeds in his mission and returns home with his prize to share (often insight or wisdom). Ultimately, the protagonist grows/changes/achieves then brings that wealth back home to alter his pre-existing everyday life. Full circle. Beginning and end mirror and contrast one another.

Circular endings must do the job of showing the hero's "homecoming", how she is changed through the turning point in the middle of the story, and what she has brought to the ordinary world to change it.

Linear Endings

Linear stories and their endings run more like a marathon up a hill, with slides, diversions and hard climbs, until they reach the summit and climax (the highest point of conflict—and resolution). Once the result of the conflict is achieved, the story is at an end. Most straight adventure stories are of this type.

Should Endings Show or Tell?

"As a fiction writer, I find endings one of the most difficult aspects of the craft," writes Erika Dreifus, short-story author and editor. "As often as we see how-to articles advising us on ways to begin stories and novels, comparable suggestions for endings are far less plentiful." she adds. This is possibly because, as Roy Peter Clark (author of

Writing Tools: 50 Essential Strategies for Every Writer) notes, "It's not easy to write about endings. To appreciate a great ending, you need to experience the whole work. Disembodied endings can seem like uprooted trees, ripped from their life source."

Roy Peter Clark reflects that "great endings bring back the whole story." He cites the "reflective ending" of *The Great Gatsby*, in which the narrator reflects back, pulling together the important narrative threads like a master weaver, to make meaningful conclusions.

"A powerful alternative," adds Clark, "is the 'narrative ending', a final scene that crowns the action." Both types of ending work when masterfully handled. The former is essentially "telling" and the latter is essentially "showing". You choose. Both work.

References

Clark, Roy Peter. 2008. *Writing Tools: 50 Essential Strategies for Every Writer*. Little, Brown and Company. 272pp.

Dibell, Ansen. 1999. *Elements of Fiction Writing: Plot*. Writer's Digest Books. Cincinnati, Ohio. 170pp.

Neal, Elsa. 2008. "Showing versus Telling—some examples". In: *Fiction Writing Side* of Bella Online, http://www.bellaonline.com/articles/art47547.asp

Wood, Monica. 1999. *Elements of Fiction Writing: Description*. Writer's Digest Books. Cincinnati, Ohio. 176pp.

F. ♥ Finding Your Muse...and Keeping It

O Muses, O high genius, aid me now!
O memory that engraved the things I saw,
Here shall your worth be manifest to all!
—Dante Alighieri, *Canto II, Inferno*

I often get asked how and from where I draw my inspiration. How do I find my muse? And how do I keep it? (And what I'm really being asked is: how do I defeat "writer's block"?).

What Is a Muse Anyway?

The Muses, in Greek mythology, are a sisterhood of goddesses or spirits who embody the arts and inspire through writing, music and dance.

Greek *mousa* (from which muse derives) means "song" or "poem". According to Pindar, to "carry a *mousa*" is "to sing a song". In ancient times, before books were common, this was the major form of learning. The first book on astronomy was set in dactylic hexameter, as were many works of pre-Socratic philosophy. Plato included philosophy as a sub-species of *mousike*.

Herodotus named each one of the nine books of his Histories after a different Muse. During the

55

late Hellenistic period, the muses were assigned standardized divisions of poetry and art. Wikipedia introduces the nine canonical Muses as:

- **Calliope** (beautiful of speech): chief of the muses and the muse of epic or heroic poetry
- **Clio** (glorious one): muse of history
- **Erato** (amorous one): muse of love or erotic poetry, lyrics and marriage songs
- **Euterpe** (well-pleasing): muse of music and lyric poetry
- **Melpomene** (chanting one): muse of tragedy
- **Polyhynmia** (singer of many hymns): muse of sacred song, oratory, lyric, singing and rhetoric
- **Terpishore** (one who delights in dance): muse of choral song and dance
- **Thalia** (blossoming one): muse of comedy and bucolic poetry
- **Urania** (celestial one): muse of astronomy

The British poet Robert Graves popularized the concept of the Muse-poet in modern times based on medieval troubadours, who celebrated the concept of courtly love.

But what IS one's muse? And how can you summon it (when you need it)?

Well, it's a little like catching a Bandersnatch.

The Journeying Muse & Defeating Writer's Block

Let's start with the opposite: many writers complain of experiencing writer's block at some point in their career—that affliction of not accessing one's creativity, when the muses have all fled to Tahiti or someplace far away and you are left with a blank page or more importantly—and alarmingly—a blank mind. No desperate search, hot shower, long walk or discussion with a friend will seduce those holidaying muses back. You're still stuck on page 49.

Here's my solution: *simply let go.* Embrace the emptiness and something wonderful will fill it. I said *something;* not necessarily what you expect. I believe that when your muse leaves you, it is on a journey. More to the point *you* are on a journey. You're living. More often  than not, our directed muse leaves us because something has gotten in the way. What you probably need to do is pay attention to that something. It's telling you something. Ironically, by doing this, you open yourself to something wonderful. Okay, enough of *somethings!*

I'm a scientist with an environmental consulting firm and my boss used to tell me that consulting was a lot like catching fish; if you weren't actually fishing you needed to cut bait. Both were critical to the whole act of catching a fish. Writing is a lot like fishing. In order to write you need something to write about. So, when the world gets in your way, you should pay attention. This is what you're here for. A writer is an artist who reports on her society. A good artist, at least an accessible one, needs to be both participant as well as observer. So, take a break and live. Chances are, you will have much more to write about after you do.

Some Muses are Harder to Invoke Than Others

In over twenty years of writing both fiction and non-fiction I really hadn't given much thought to writer's block until recently, when I was challenged on it. This is not to say that I never experienced it. I did; I just kept on writing.

"What?" you say. "Then, you didn't really have writer's block." Well, I did, but only for that particular project, and only for one aspect of that particular project. The key is to have multiple projects and recognize that each of these has multiple tasks aside from writing (e.g., editing, research, discussion, etc.) that you can work on.

For instance, besides Novel A, whose plot had me stumped, I was working on two short stories and a non-fiction article. I was also actively posting science articles, essays and opinion pieces on my blog. In addition, I was writing news articles for an online magazine and doing my regular stint at the environmental consulting firm, writing interpretive environmental reports. I kept on writing.

I let the plot of Novel A sit for a while as I continued to write. That didn't mean I couldn't work on Novel A in other capacities: copy editing or polishing language, for instance. The point I want to make is that it's helpful to have other things on the go mainly because this will let you relax about the project that has you stumped. And you need to relax for it to resolve. It's a little like looking for the watch you mis-placed; it will find you once you stop looking for it.

Letting the Muse Return (on its own terms)

Each of you has felt it: that otherworldly, euphoric wave of "knowing", of resonating with something that is more than the visible world: when the hairs on the back of your neck tingle as you write that significant scene...or trembling with giddy energy as you create that perfect line on a painting...or glowing with a deep abiding warmth when you defend a principle... or the surging frisson you share with fellow musicians on that exquisite set piece...or the cresting orgasm with your cherished lover. These are all what I call God moments. And they don't happen by chasing after them; they sneak up on us when we're not looking. They come to us when we focus outward and embrace our wonder for this world. When we quiet our minds and nurture our souls with beauty (see Chapter Z).

Wake Up The Sleeping Muse

Here are a few things that help me entice those capricious muses into action:

Music: music moves me in inexplicable ways. I use music to inspire my muse. Every book has its thematic music, which I play while I write and when I drive to and from work (where I do my best plot/theme thinking). I even go so far as to have a musical theme for each character.

Walks: despite what I said above, going for a walk, particularly in a natural environment, un-cluttered with human-made distractions, also unclutters the mind and soul. It grounds you back to the simplicity of life.

Cycling: a favorite way to clear my mind is to cycle (I think any form of exercise would suffice); just getting your heart rate up and pumping those endorphins through you soothes the soul and unleashes the brain to freely run the field.

Attend writers' functions: go to the library and listen to a writer read from her work. You never know how it might inspire you. Browse the bookshelves of the library or bookstore. Attend a writers' convention or conference.

Visit an art gallery, go to a movie: art of any kind can inspire creativity. Fine art is open to interpretation and can provoke your mind in ways you hadn't thought. If you go with an appreciative friend and discuss what you've seen you add another element to the experience.

Go on a trip with a friend: tour the city or, better yet, take a road trip with a good friend or alone (if you are comfortable with it). I find that travelling is a great way to help me focus outward, forget myself, and open my mind and soul to adventure and learning something new. Road trips are metaphoric journeys of the soul.

Form a writers' group: sharing ideas with people of like mind (or not, but of respectful mind) can both inspire you and provide the seeds of ideas.

References

Robert Graves, 1948. *The White Goddess, a historical grammar of poetic myth.* Faber & Faber. UK. 535pp.

Wikipedia. 2008. Muse. http://en.wikipedia.org/wiki/Muses

G. ● Defining Your Genre & Going Beyond It

Great fleas have little fleas upon their backs to bite 'em, And little fleas have lesser fleas, and so ad infinitum. And the great fleas themselves, in turn, have greater fleas to go on; While these again have greater still, and greater still, and so on
—A. De Morgan, *Budget of Paradoxes*

Our multiplex world of discerning consumers is getting used to having what they consume laid out clearly and categorized. Literature is no different. Since the time of the ancient Greeks, when Aristotle proclaimed in his *Poetics* that poetry could be categorized into many species, critics have endeavored to label art to help the "commoner" interpret it.

What Is "Genre" & Is It Useful?

The word "genre" comes from the French word for "kind" or "gender" and provides a loose set of criteria for a category of composition. People in the book industry often use it to categorize literature.

"Genre" is notoriously difficult to define. For instance, what kinds of literary form should properly be called genres? Poetry is generally thought of as a literary "mode", being too broad and too varied to be called a "genre". The various types and forms of poetry are more properly called genres, such as the *epic* or the *lyric.*

A genre can be defined either by the formal properties of the work, or by its subject matter. A poem can be called a *sonnet* if it is fourteen lines long, or described as an *elegy* if it speaks of the death of a loved or admired person.

Although genres are not precisely definable, genre considerations are one of the most important factors in determining what a person will see or read. Many genres have built-in audiences and corresponding publications that support them, such as magazines and websites. Some people think that books and movies that are difficult to categorize into a genre are likely to be less successful commercially. They're probably right.

So, if you haven't figured out what genre your writing falls under, start figuring it out now; your future publisher and marketer will want to know because they, in turn, have to tell their distributor and bookseller where to shelve the book. This is why *you* need to do this, no matter what you think of categorizing your work; the alternative is leaving it to Jack in the marketing department who may not have even read your book, but used the cover picture to figure it out. Yikes!

Today's Teacher provides the following list for genres in literature:

- Biography/Autobiography
- Fantasy
- Historical Fiction
- Myths & Legends
- Poetry
- Science Fiction
- Fairy Tales
- Folk Tales
- Mystery
- Realistic Fiction
- Non-Fiction
- Short Stories

They were pretty good in identifying the major genres but they missed Romance, Westerns, Horror, Erotica, Literary Fiction, Humor, and Young Adult (if you want to call that a genre). The point I'm making is that each person is bound to come up with a different list of genre categories. Go to five of your favorite bookstores (not just the chain stores, but the independent bookstores) and see for yourself how the professionals do it. It's a miserable confusing mess. I've seen science fiction thrown in with fantasy and the whole category called fantasy. I've seen Diana Gabaldon's historical time traveler series shelved under romance, main-stream and science fiction or fantasy depending on the bookstore. In truth, it's all of these. Which brings us to cross-genre literature. But I'm getting ahead of myself. First, let's look at the sub-categories...

Subgenres Too

Genres are often divided into complex sub-categories. The novel is a large genre of narrative fiction; within the category of the novel, the detective novel is a subgenre while the hard-boiled detective novel is a subgenre of the detective novel. *And so ad infinitum...*

Wikipedia tells us that literature can be divided into three basic kinds—the classic genres of Ancient Greece: poetry, drama, and prose. Poetry may then be subdivided into epic, lyric, and dramatic. Comedy has subgenres that include farce, comedy of manners, burlesque, and satire. And it goes on.

The Hierarchy of Genres & Subgenre Categories

For example, let's take a genre I'm very familiar with—science fiction—and break it down. Science fiction has recognized subgenres that include hard or soft science fiction, with specific definitions to go with each. The term speculative fiction was coined by SF author Robert A. Heinlein as an umbrella term that covers all genres that depict alternate realities. Even fiction on faster-than-light travel is still considered science fiction, because science is a main subject in the work.

Marg Gilks and Moira Allen do a stunning job of listing the major subgenres of science fiction, which include, in addition to those that I've included:

- **Alternate history** (e.g., Harry Turtledove's *Guns of the South*)
- **Apocalyptic, holocaust, and post-apocalyptic** (e.g., Niven and Pournelle's *Lucifer's Hammer* or Nevil Shute's *On the Beach*)
- **Cross-genre** (e.g., Linnea Sinclair's *Shades of Dark*)
- **Cyberpunk** (e.g., William Gibson's *Neuromancer*)
- **First contact** (e.g., H.G. Wells' *War of the Worlds*)
- **Hard science fiction** (e.g., Isaac Asimov's *I, Robot*)
- **Light/humorous science fiction** (e.g., Douglas Adams' *Hitchhiker's Guide to the Galaxy*)
- **Military science fiction** (e.g., Robert Heinlein's *Starship Troopers*)
- **Near-future science fiction** (e.g., Greg Bear's *Blood Music*)
- **Science fantasy/future fantasy** (e.g., Edgar Rice Burroughs' *Barsoom* novels)
- **Sociological/political fantasy** (e.g., Elizabeth Haydon's *The Symphony of Ages*)
- **Slipstream** (e.g., Margaret Atwood's *The Handmaid's Tale*)
- **Soft/sociological science fiction** (e.g., Robert Silverberg's short story *To See the Invisible Man*, Ursula K. LeGuin's *Left Hand of Darkness*)

- **Space opera** (e.g., George Lukas' *Star Wars*)
- **Time travel** (e.g., H.G. Wells' *The Time Machine*)
- **Alternate universe** (e.g., Philip Pullman's *His Dark Materials*)

Anyone who is familiar with the science fiction genre will spot where I've left some category out. I'm reminded of the taxonomic work I conducted early in my career as an aquatic ecologist. There are "splitters" and "lumpers" and the two shall never meet.

Slipstream: Those Pesky "Cross-Genre" Pieces...

"Cross-genre", also called "slipstream" or "interstitial fiction" or "fabulation", is most commonly defined as fiction that crosses genre boundaries. Unless you're Bruce Sterling, that is, who defines slipstream as:

> *A contemporary kind of writing which has set its face against consensus reality. It is fantasic, surreal sometimes, speculative on occasion, but not rigorously so. It does not aim to provoke a 'sense of wonder' or to systematically extrapolate in the manner of classic science fiction. Instead, this is a kind of writing that simply makes you feel very strange; the way that living in the later twentieth century makes you feel, if you are a person of a certain sensibility. We could call this kind of fiction Novels of*

Postmodern Sensibility, but that looks pretty bad on a category rack, and requires an acronym besides; so for the sake of convenience and argument, we will call these books 'slipstream.'

...Simply makes you feel strange? Although lots of writing may do that to me (of course, I'm strange already), I'm not sure that I would define slipstream as writing that "makes you feel strange". This is because I don't think you can pin it down; it's too slippery a creature (examples include: Margaret Atwood's *Oryx and Crake*; Bruce Sterling's *The Little Magic Shop*). However, I think that this form (or is it a *movement?*) is promising to be one of the most exciting things occurring in literature today.

James Patrick Kelly, in *Asimov's Science Fiction*, wrote:

> Today, we have literally many dozens of writers in both mainstream and genre who are working from these influences and creating new forms of cross-pollination. The problem with talking about cross-genre is that it's not a single movement—it's a bunch of individual writers pursuing individual visions that tend to simply share some of the same diverse influences. So it's difficult to pin down and say 'this is what it is and what it isn't.' That's what is exciting to me about it—that it is difficult to categorize. In a sense, that means it's a complex, organic creature.

Some popular "cross-genre" mixes include:

- Action comedy = action + comedy
- Black comedy (tragicomedy) = tragedy + comedy
- Comedy-drama (dramedy) = comedy + drama
- Romantic comedy = romance + comedy
- Science fantasy = science fiction + fantasy
- Science fiction Western = science fiction + western
- Weird West = western + any mix of: horror/sci-fi/speculative fiction/steampunk/superheroes

A friend of mine who is part Cree writes slipstream or cross-genre works that are essentially unclassifiable. Although she is a tremendous writer, she has yet to find a publisher. I know why; they don't know how to market her books to the booksellers. Where do you put them on the bookshelf? What a conundrum.

But, things are changing and hopefully my friend will see the results of that change. The irony of slipstream defying categorization is that it may be the next bestseller.

"From the 'Lord of the Rings' box-office smashes in the theaters to adults reading 'Harry Potter' books on their commute, it seems that the fantasy genre has permeated the mainstream," notes Alana Abott, of Thomson Gale (an e-research and educational publishing firm). "The publishing industry has noticed, and new books combining familiar mainstream forms such as historical fiction, romance, and chick-lit are beginning to see an influx of magic." Cross-pollination is cool. Cross-genre is in.

References

Abott, Alana. 2006. "Cross-Genre Fairy Godmother" In: Literature Community News, http://www.gale.cengage.com/articles/2006/06/cross-genre

Gilks, Marg, and Moira Allen. 2003. "The Subgenres of Science Fiction" In: http://www.writing-world.com/sf/genres.shtml

Robert Graves, 1999. The White Goddess, a historical grammar of poetic myth. Faber & Faber. 2Rev Ed. 535pp.

Kelly, James Patrick. 2008. "On the Net: Slipstream". In: Asimov's Science Fiction, http://www.asimovs.com/ issue 0312/onthenet.shtml

Today's Teacher: http://www.todaysteacher.com/LiteratureGenreList.htm

MSN.Encarta. 2008. "Literary Genre". In: http://uk.encarta.msn.com/encyclopedia 781533585/Genre (literature).html

Wikepedia. 2008. "Genre". In: http://en.wikipedia.org/wiki/Genre

H. ● House or Home...
Creating Memorable Settings

Place Your Story

Every story has a few important characters doing important things, each enacting his or her story. "Put all the stories together and you [have] at their center a portrait of a place," says Richard Russo, acclaimed novelist. Setting includes time, place and circumstance of a story.

Setting fulfills most of the core aspects of a story. Without a place there is no story. Setting serves multipurpose roles from helping with plot, determining and describing character to providing metaphoric links to theme. Setting, like the force in *Star Wars*, provides a landscape that binds everything into context and meaning. Without setting, characters are simply there, in a vacuum, with no reason to act and most importantly, no reason to care.

"Man...is a creature of his environment," wrote Robert Louis Stevenson. "His outlook on life will be colored by the setting in which he is placed."

"If you're not writing stories that occur in a specific place," adds Russo, "you're missing an opportunity to add depth and character to your writing."

71

Setting as Character

Settings can not only *have* character; they can *be* a character in their own right. A novelist may often find herself, when portraying several characters, painting a portrait of place. This is setting being "character". The setting functions as a catalyst, and molds the more traditional characters that animate a story. Think of any of your favorite books, particularly the epics: *The Wizard of Oz, Tale of Two Cities, Doctor Zhivago, Lord of the Rings, The Odyssey*, etc. In each of these books the central character is really the place, which is inexorably linked to its main character. How much is Frodo, for instance, an extension of his beloved Shire? They are one in the same, in fact. Just as the London of Charles Dickens spawned Scrooge. Or Hardy's Egdon Heath  shaped Eustacia Vye in *The Return of the Native*. D.H. Lawrence suggested that the heath was the most important character in Hardy's book:

> *Egdon, whose dark soil was strong and crude and organic as the body of a beast.*

Setting, then, comes to mean so much more. Setting ultimately portrays what lies at the heart of the story.

Setting as Metaphor

Settings depict the theme of your story through metaphor. Richard Russo says, "to know the rhythms, the textures, the feel of a place is to know more deeply and truly its people." Place is destiny. Russo asserts that for fiction writers place is crucial to human destiny and the formation of human personality. He adds, "The more specific and individual things become, the more universal they feel." This is not an oxymoron, but an example of the principle of a truism, which primary comes to us in the form of a paradox.

An example of the importance of place in a story is provided by E. Annie Proux's *The Shipping News*. Her protagonist, Quoyle, displays a self-conscious gesture of covering his strong native chin with his hand until he returns from New York to his homeland, Newfoundland, where he can live a natural and graceful life without apology.

Settings can be used very effectively to depict characters. Think of it. The setting and all the objects in it are described to your reader through your POV character. This gives you an excellent opportunity to show the mood, temperament, judgment and bias of your character.

Setting & Structure

To reiterate, the components of setting include: 1) time, 2) place and 3) circumstance.

All three form a kind of critical mass that creates the particular setting best suited to your story.

Juggle any one of these and they will affect the quality of the other. Circumstance, in particular, modifies the nature of time and place. For instance, let's take the bucolic setting of Booker Ranch in Kentucky set in the 1930s. Now, let's add circumstance: 1) The Booker Ranch is threatened with receivership; or 2) Amy Booker's estranged husband returns to the ranch just as she gives birth to a baby boy or 3) George Booker's horse, *Makeamillion*, wins the Kentucky Derby in Louisville. In each case the time and place remain the same but the circumstance gives the setting its unique flavor.

Circumstance may be expressed at the character level (e.g., John just lost his job), environmental level (e.g., the community is getting nervous), or global level (e.g., the world economy just crashed). Science fiction writer James Alan Gardner provides an example of setting under differing large-scale circumstances:

1. Global warming has melted the polar ice caps and much of Manhattan is under water. The city is mostly abandoned, left to lowlifes and criminals.

2. Same environmental condition, except the city isn't abandoned; instead, it becomes a kind of "Venice" with gondolas drifting down Broadway.

3. Same environmental condition, except that aliens intervene, making all humans their slaves; the city is a prison camp.

You get the picture, or setting, rather. "As a writer, you should set the circumstances to your advantage," says Gardner. For instance, "would a particular scene be more effective in a rainstorm or in pleasant weather?" The details of setting can enhance, contradict or give a unique flavor to your scene, your characters in the scene and ultimately your story.

Looking Inside

Good examples of interior settings can be found in *The Glass Menagerie*, Scott Fitzgerald's *The Great Gatsby* and, according to Russo, Mary Gordon's *The Important Houses*. In Gordon's story, "we get a marvelous sense of character despite the fact that we never meet any of the people," says Russo. The contents provide a rich portrait of its owner:

> *...every object in her house belonged to the Old World. Nothing was easy; everything required maintenance of a complicated and specialized sort...*

I still vividly recall the opening scene of the film version of Scott Fitzgerald's *The Great Gatsby*: the camera slowly panning a sweeping view of the opulent interior of Gatsby's house.

Looking Outside

"The relationship between character and her exterior setting is more mysterious," says Russo, because your character doesn't "own" a landscape or a street or a neighborhood. For this reason, Russo contends that novice writers tend to underplay exterior setting.

To Russo's question "Where does this story take place?" he's often heard: "it's really more about the *people.*" If the story is set in a vague urban place, he asks, "which city are we in?" and is told, "It doesn't really matter; it's *every* city." But, the irony is, we do want to know. It grounds us as a reader into the real world. It helps the story resonate with a "sense of place"; something we all want to have for ourselves.

I've been told that editors tend to have little faith in the vision of writers who don't clearly depict the world their characters inhabit (see Chapter A on World Building). Imagine Thomas Hardy's characters without Egdon Heath; or George Eliot's Maggie Tulliver without St Ogg.

Setting & Emotion

The setting may amplify a character's emotions or contradict them, depending on the circumstance of your character, her mood, disposition, tendencies and observational skills. Either way, setting provides an emotional landscape upon which a character's own temperament may play counterpoint or may resonate in a wonderful symphony. Always think of the less obvious; think of contrast and how you can increase tension and emphasize the character's situation.

For instance, if your character has just moved upstate from the south and is homesick, you could have the setting be her ally as it commiserates and shares her misery by weeping rain. Or…provide an otherwise cheerful setting of bright azure sky and brilliant fall colors that plays the role of villain, its empty crispness mocking her sadness and her ache for the rich warm smells of home: even the weather doesn't share her misery; she is utterly alone.

Setting as Weather

Weather, more than any other aspect of a character's environment, can convey the mood and tone of both story and character. Rain. Storms. Darkness. Wind. Scorching sun. These all convey many things in story. They are not just part of the scenery; they are devices in plot and theme. Think of Michael Ondaatje's *The English Patient* and how he used the desert setting and the hot winds to evoke mood, character, tension, theme and ultimately story.

> *The desert could not be claimed or owned—it was a piece of cloth carried by winds, never held down by stones, and given a hundred shifting names long before Canterbury existed, long before battles and treaties quilted Europe and the East*
> —The English Patient

Another example of "wind" as strong metaphor to evoke theme is the opening in Joanne Harris's *Chocolat*:

> *We came on the wind of the carnival. A warm wind for February, laden with the hot greasy scents of frying pancakes and sausages and powdery-sweet waffles cooked on the*

77

hot plate right there by the roadside
—Chocolat

Be mindful not to overdo the use of weather as metaphor. Some uses have become overdone, cliché (e.g., the dark storm of impending doom). Avoid the obvious. Be creative. Be subtle. Use contrast. And remember to show rather than tell. In an article for *Articlesbase*, Mark Walton suggests you focus on the changing light, textures, sounds and smells when considering the phenomenon of rain to help convey story.

When you're doing your research, make sure you get your facts straight; don't place a hurricane in a location it never occurs, unless it's meant to be an oddity.

Some Cool Tips

Author and creative writing teacher Carolyn Oravitz suggests the following:

- Don't tack setting in; make it an integral part of the story
- Describe selectively and with purpose—through integration in scene rather than exposition (see Chapter E)
- Be specific (e.g., soft pink rose, not flower; beat up Chevy, not car; old clapboard cottage, not house
- Use similes, metaphors, personification to describe setting
- Use the senses like sight, sound, smell, taste, feel
- Don't tell, show (e.g., don't say the time is the 1940s; show the cars, radios, dresses. Don't tell the reader it's raining; show them by describing the dripping trees, etc.)
- Compare and contrast settings and relate them to

the POV characters

- Don't describe setting all at once in the beginning, work it in slowly throughout the story

Exercise:

1. Write about a public place from your childhood that inspires powerful emotions. Describe it from as many senses as you can remember.

2. Describe a place through the POV of character #1 (with a certain mood and temperament); now describe the same place through the eyes of character #2 (who is different from #1). Use vivid language and try to bring in as many senses as possible. Now compare.

3. Have one character describe a place or object that belongs to a second character. Is it full of new things or old things? Is it tidy or a mess? Is it dark or bright? Cluttered or empty?

References

Gardner, James Alan. 2001. "A Seminar on Writing Prose". In: *Writing Advice*, http://www.thinkage.ca/~jim/advice.html.

Oravitz, Carolyn. 2007. "Where and When". In: *Writing Workshop Series/Setting*. The Independent.

Russo, Richard. 1999. "Location, Location, Location: Depicting Character Through Place" In: *Fiction Writer*. April, 1999.

Walton, Mark. 2008. "One Mistake To Avoid In Setting The Scene In Your Novel, Is To Overlook The Weather". In: *Articlesbase*, http://www.articlesbase.com/writing-articles/one-mistake-to-avoid-in-setting

I. ☻ Interviews and Other Weird Experiences

Being a Smart Reporter

The pillars of good journalism include:

- thoroughness
- accuracy
- fairness and
- transparency.

These days, **thoroughness** means more than exhausting your resources, real or virtual. It also includes getting input from your readers, says Robin Good, online publisher and new media communication expert.

Likewise, says Good, being **accurate** may include saying what you don't know and being open to input from your readership; this invites dialogue between you and your respected reader. The key, of course, is respect.

Which brings us to **fairness**: this includes listening to different viewpoints and incorporating them into your journalism. Fairness, says Good, is about letting people respond and listening to them, particularly if they disagree with you. Both learn from the experience.

And, lastly, part of being **transparent** is to reveal and make accessible to your readers your source material.

Things to Consider When Doing That Interview

As a writer of either fiction or non-fiction, you will at some time require information from a real person. Depending on the nature of your research and its intended destination and audience, you may wish to conduct anything from a casual phone or email enquiry to a full-blown formal face-to-face interview. This will also depend on who you are interviewing, from a neighbor to a government official.

In an article in *Writer's Digest* (February, 2008) Joy Lanzendorfer suggests that you adopt the following tactics to get your interview further than the basics and to fully take advantage of your source (oh, I didn't mean it *that* way!):

- **Do your research ahead of time**: read up on your subject and include both sides of an issue (if that's relevant). This helps you to respond intelligently with better follow-up questions.

- **Ask open-ended questions**: avoid yes and no questions and get them to elaborate. Asking "why" solicits explanation, which will give your article depth.

- **Ask for examples**: this provides a personal aspect to the article that gives it warmth and makes it more interesting.

- **Ask personal questions**: what's the worst thing that can happen? They can simply say no; the up side is you may get a gem. The personal angle from the interviewee's perspective gives your article some potential emotional aspect that gives it human-interest.

- **Ask the interviewee for any further thoughts to share**: it's an innocuous question, but can offer-up more gems. What it provides you with is the possibility of getting something you might not have thought of, sparked by your conversation.

What NOT to Say...

Nancie Hudson gives the following excellent advice about what you should never say to a source in an article in *Writer's Digest* (April, 2007):

- **"There's no rush."** Never reveal your deadline. Think about it; what do you normally do when there's a deadline? Right...say it's sooner than it really is.

- **"I've never covered this topic before."** This kind of information is inappropriate and may make your interviewee uncomfortable (worrying about your un-proven abilities to properly interview her instead of focusing on herself). Besides, it's not what you know but what you learn that counts.

- **"I'll be using what you say exten-sively."** Don't assume and make prom-ises you may not be able to keep, until *after* the interview.

- **"I don't get it."** If you don't understand something, get clari-fication rather than make a negative remark that tends to stop them dead in their tracks.

- **"You can review the piece before it's published."** This is something that can be dealt with over the phone to confirm facts; the source doesn't need to see the whole piece before it's published.

- **"This is going to be a fantastic article!"** Keep your tone professional; there's nothing wrong with being positive, but you should maintain a professional attitude that inspires confidence in the interviewee.

References

Good, Robin. "The Pillars of Good Journalism". In: Master New Media:
http://www.masternewmedia.org/news/2005/01/29/the_pillars_of_good_journalism

Hudson, Nancie. 2007. "6 Things You Should Never Say to a Source". In: *Writer's Digest*. April, 2007.

Lanzendorfer, Joy. 2008. "Interview Tactics". In: *Writer's Digest*. February, 2008.

J. ☻ A Hero's Journey

Midway upon the journey of our life I found myself within a forest dark, For the straightforward pathway had been lost
　—Dante Alighieri (*Divine Comedy*)

Summoned or not, the god will come
　—motto over the door of Carl Jung's house

According to Christopher Vogler (author of *The Writer's Journey: Mythic Structure for Writers*) "all stories consist of a few common structural elements found universally in myths, fairy tales, dreams, and movies. They are known collectively as **The Hero's Journey.**" The Hero's Journey is essentially the three-act structure of the ancient Greek play, according to Ridley Pearson (*Writer's Digest*, 2007). The three-act structure was handed down to us thousands of years ago and consists of Beginning, Middle, and End (otherwise known as Opening, Development, Conclusion or "the decision to act", "the action" and "the consequences of the action").

Dating from before history, the Hero's Journey duplicates the steps of the rite of passage and is a process of self-discovery and self-integration. The Hero's Journey is a concept drawn from the depth psychology of Swiss psychologist Carl

Jung and the scholar and mythologist Joseph Campbell, author of *The Hero with a Thousand Faces*. Jung proposed that symbols appear to us when there is a need to express what thought cannot think or what is only divined or felt. Jung discovered reoccurring symbols among differing peoples and cultures, unaffected by time and space. He described these shared symbols as

archetypes which are irepressible, unconscious, preexisting forms of the inherited structure of the psyche and manifested themselves spontaneously anywhere, anytime. Joseph Campbell suggested that these mythic images lay at the depth of the unconscious where humans are no longer distinct individuals, where our minds widen and merge into the mind of humankind. Where we are all the same.

In his book, *The Hero with a Thousand Faces*, Campbell articulated the life principles embedded in the structure of stories. He recognized that myths weren't just abstract theories or quaint ancient beliefs but practical models for understanding how to live. Ultimately, the hero's journey is the soul's search for home. It is a long and tortuous journey of the soul seeking enlightenment-redemption-salvation only to find it by returning "home" (though, often not the home previously envisioned). It is a journey we all take, in some form.

Heroes are agents of change. Joseph Campbell

defines the hero as "the champion not of things to become but of things becoming; the dragon to be slain by him is precisely the monster of the status quo; Holdfast the keeper of the past." The hero's task has always been to bring new life to an ailing culture, says Carol S. Pearson, author of *The Hero Within.*

Christopher Vogler tells us that writers are "storytellers." He says that "the best of them have utilized the principles of myth to create masterful stories that are dramatic, entertaining, and psychologically true." Vogler goes on to say that "the Hero's Journey is not an invention, but an observation. It is a recognition of a beautiful design, a set of principles that govern the conduct of life and the world of storytelling the way physics and chemistry govern the physical world." He likens the Hero's Journey to an eternal reality, a Platonic ideal form, a divine model. He says "that the Hero's Journey is nothing less than a handbook for life, a complete instruction manual in the art of being human." This is why the Hero's Journey model for writing is so relevant; because it appeals to all readers. We are all on a journey.

Mystic Annie Dillard, in her book *Pilgrim at Tinker Creek,* offers that life "is often cruel, but always beautiful—the least we can do is try to be there." To be fully in life. The universe," says Dillard, "was not made in jest but in solemn, incomprehensible earnest. By a power that is unfathomably secret, and holy, and fleet. There is nothing to be done about it, but ignore it, or see."

Pearson adds, "The emerging heroic ideal does not see life as a challenge to be overcome, but a gift to be received."

The Hero's Journey in Myth & Fiction

In some versions of the *Holy Grail* story, relates Pearson, the hero reaches a huge chasm with no apparent way to get across to the Grail castle. The space is too great for him to jump across. Then he remembers the Grail teaching that instructs him to step out in faith. As he puts one foot out into the abyss, a bridge magically appears and he is saved.

Sir Launcelot

Anyone who has left a job, school, or a relationship has stepped out into that abyss, separating them from the familiar world they've known.

Just as "the knights of King Arthur's Round Table set off to seek the Holy Grail," says Mary Henderson, author of *Star Wars: The Magic of Myth*, "the great figures of every major religion have each gone on a 'vision quest', from Moses' journey to the mountain, to Jesus' time in the desert, Muhammad's mediations in the mountain cave, and Buddha's search for enlightenment that ended under the Bodhi tree."

The journey, and the abyss, is often not a physical adventure, adds Henderson, but a spiritual one, "as the hero moves from ignorance and innocence to experience and enlightenment."

The Hero's Journey Map

Table 1 shows Vogler's twelve-stage description of the three-act storyline, based on Campbell's eight-step transformation model.

Table 1: The Hero's Journey Map

Act One: Separation	
Ordinary World	Describes the Hero's world with its problems and how the hero may or may not quite fit in.
Call to Adventure	the **herald** presents the hero with a problem, challenge and/or adventure; irrevocably changing the ordinary world.
Refusal of the Call	Our reluctant hero balks at the threshold of adventure.
Meeting with the Mentor	The **mentor** provides the hero with a gift to help her through the threshold.
Crossing the Threshold	The hero commits to the adventure and enters the Special World.
Act Two: Initiation & Transformation	
Tests, Allies, Enemies	The hero must face tests, makes allies and enemies and begins to learn the rules of the Special World.

Approach to the Inmost Cave	The hero reaches the edge of the most dangerous place, often where the object of her quest resides.
Ordeal (the Abyss)	Our hero hits bottom, where she faces "death" and is on the brink of battle with the most powerful hostile force
Reward/seizing the sword (Transformation & Revelation)	Having survived "death" (of fear or ignorance) our hero—and the reader—receives a reward or elixir in the form of an epiphany and transforms.

Act Three: The Return

The Road Block	Our hero must deal with the consequences of confronting the dark forces of the Ordeal (e.g., chase scene).
Resurrection/Atonement	The hero is transformed in this climactic moment through her experience and seeks atonement with her reborn self, now in harmony with the "new" world; the imbalance which sent her on her journey, mostly corrected or path made clear.
Return with the Elixir	Our hero returns to the Ordinary World with some elixir, treasure or lesson from the Special World.

The Archetypes

The world of fairy tales and myth (which most stories use in some form) is peopled with recurring character types and relationships. Heroes on a quest, heralds and wise old men or women who provide them with "gifts", shady fellow-travelers—threshold guardians—who may "block" the path, tricksters who confuse and complicate things and evil villains who simply want to destroy our hero. Jung adopted the term **archetypes**, which means ancient patterns of personality shared by humanity, to describe these as a **collective unconscious**. This is what makes these archetypes, or symbols, so important to the storyteller. Assigning an archetype to a character allows the writer to clarify that character's role in the story as well as to determine the overall theme of the story itself. Archetypes are therefore an important tool in the universal language of storytelling, just as myth serves the overall purpose of supplying "the symbols that carry the human spirit forward." (Joseph Campbell).

Joseph Campbell went so far as to describe the archetype as something that is expressed biologically and is wired into every human being. Before I introduce you to the principal archetypes as described by Joseph Campbell and Christopher Vogler, it is important for you to understand that an archetype need not be fixed; that is, a particular character may evolve and function through several archetypes. This makes characters more real, interesting and less allegorical.

Vogler lists the seven useful archetypes:

- Hero
- Mentor
- Herald
- Threshold guardian

- Shapeshifter
- Shadow
- Trickster

The Hero

Taken from the Greek root that means "to protect and to serve", a hero is someone willing to sacrifice his own needs on behalf of others.

Vogler says that the hero archetype "represents the ego's search for identity and wholeness." The hero provides a character for us to identify with. She is usually the principal POV character in a story and has qualities most readers can (or want to) identify with. This means someone with flaws (not a cardboard cutout of infinite virtue); someone like you and me. The function of the hero is to grow and change through her journey as she encounters other archetypes. Every hero is on a quest, a mission, or a journey, whether it is an actual physical journey or (and usually combined with) a psychological journey toward "home" (salvation or redemption) through sacrifice. "The true mark of the hero, says Vogler, is in the act of **sacrifice**, "the hero's willingness to give up something of value, perhaps even her own life, on behalf of an ideal or a group," and ultimately for the greater good.

Heroes may be willing or unwilling. Some can be

described as anti-heroes, notably flawed characters that must grow significantly to achieve the status of true hero. Often the anti-hero starts off behaving more like a villain, like the character Crais in *Farscape* or Tom Cruise's character in *Rain Man*. The wounded anti-hero may be a "heroic knight in tarnished armor, a loner who has rejected society or been rejected by it," according to Vogler. Examples include Jim Stark in *Rebel Without a Cause* and Aragorn in *Lord of the Rings*. The catalyst hero provides an exception to the rule of hero undergoing the most change. This type of hero shows less of a character arc (changing very little) but precipitates significant change or transformation in other protagonists. A good example is the character David Adams in Ben Bova's *Colony*.

In *Awakening the Heroes Within*, Carol S. Pearson provides further categories for hero-archetypes, including: innocent, orphan, martyr, wanderer, warrior, caregiver, seeker, lover, destroyer, creator, ruler, magician, sage, and fool. As with Vogler's archetypes, these aren't necessarily fixed for an individual hero, who may embrace several of these archetypes during his transformation in response to events and ordeals set before him.

Pearson grouped these hero-archetypes according to stages of a hero's journey and elements of his responding psyche. For instance the Ego relates to the preparation for the journey and includes: Innocent; Orphan; Warrior; and Caregiver. The Soul (the unconsciousness) relates to the journey itself and includes: Seeker; Destroyer; and Lover. The Self (individuation) relates to the return from the journey and includes: Ruler; Magician; Sage; and Fool. A hero may use any of these archetypes at various times in her life, but she can also use all of them within a day or an hour.

Table 2 shows how Pearson breaks these down into six main archetypes with associated task, plot structure and hero's "gift".

Table 2: A Hero's Role & Gift

Archetype	Task	Plot Structure	Gift
Orphan	Survive difficulty	How she suffered & survived	Resilience
Wanderer	Find herself	How she escaped & found her way	Independence
Warrior	Prove her worth	How she achieved her goals	Courage
Altruist	Show generosity	How she gave to others	Compassion
Innocent	Achieve happiness	How she found the promised land	Faith
Magician	Transform herself	How she changed the world	power

The Mentor

The word mentor comes to us from Homer's *The Odyssey*, after a character who guides Telemachus on his hero's journey. The mentor is usually a positive figure who aids or trains the hero. The mentor often possesses divine wisdom and has faith in the hero and shows great enthusiasm, as a result. The word "enthusiasm" itself means god-inspired or having a god in you. The mentor represents the "Self", the god within us, says Vogler; a higher Self that is wiser, nobler and more godlike.

The mentor often gives the hero a "**gift**"—once the hero has earned it, that is. The gift is usually something important for the hero's use on his journey; either a weapon to destroy a "monster" or a "talisman" to enlighten the hero in deciding the path of her journey. A good example of this is in *Star Wars*, when Luke's mentor, Obi Wan, provides him with his father's lightsaber.

The mentor also serves as inventor, the hero's conscience, as motivator, or information provider. In love stories the mentor may function in the role of initiation. Vogler describes many types of mentor from fallen mentors to dark mentors, shamans, and comics.

The Herald

The herald brings in a new force, usually in Act One of the story. This force is usually a challenge for change. Heralds announce the coming of significant change, whether the hero likes it or not (and usually s/he doesn't).

In Act One, we usually find the hero struggling, getting by in her Ordinary World; yearning, like Luke Skywalker on Tatooine, for "more". Often not even realizing it. The herald is a new energy, a catalyst that enters the story and makes it impossible for the hero to remain in status quo. The herald tips the scales, so to speak. This could be in the form of a person, an event, a condition or just information that shifts the hero's balance and changes her world, as a result. Nothing will ever be the same.

The herald delivers the **call to adventure**. In *Star Wars*, Ben Kenobi, who also serves as Luke Skywalker's mentor, issues the call when he invites Luke to join him on his mission to Alderaan. The herald also provides the hero with motivation. In *Romancing the Stone*, the herald for Joan Wilder comes in the form of a treasure map in the mail, and a distressed phone call from her sister.

The Threshold Guardian

This archetype guards the threshold of "Separation from the Ordinary World" on the hero's journey to attain his "prize" and achieve his destiny. A threshold guardian is usually not the main antagonist. In the *Harry Potter* series, this role is fulfilled by Malfoy, Snape or Filch even; while the main antagonist is provided, of course, by the character of Voldemort.

Threshold guardians spice up the story by providing obstacles the hero must overcome. They help to round out the hero's journey and develop her character arc. In many cases, they may even be more interesting than the main villain. In rare cases, the threshold guardian may, in fact, be a secret helper, placed in the hero's path to test her ability and commitment to her journey. Ultimately, the role of the threshold guardian is to **test the hero** on her path.

A hero succeeds when she recognizes a threshold guardian as providing an opportunity to strengthen her powers, or resolve her will. Threshold guardians aren't defeated so much as incorporated by the hero, as she learns their tricks, absorbs them and goes on. "Ultimately", says Vogler, "fully evolved heroes feel compassion for their apparent enemies and transcend rather than destroy them."

The Shapeshifter

The shapeshifter can seem one thing and in fact be another. They are often mendacious and crafty; they add dramatic tension to the story and provide the hero with a puzzle to solve. This archetype serves as "a catalyst for change and a symbol of the psychological urge to transform", according to Vogler.

The shapeshifter brings **doubt and suspense** to the story and tests the hero's abilities to discern her path. In many cases the hero must evolve from a naivety through her interactions with this slippery character. The character of Palpatine in *Star Wars* appears good and is really evil. Even the character Yoda in *Star Wars*, is a bit of a shapeshifter, initially masking his ancient wisdom with a foolish childlike appearance when Luke first encounters him. The character that Mike Douglas plays in *Romancing the Stone* appears as a shapeshifter to Joan Wilder until the very end of the story. Till the very end she was asking herself: Is he my ally or my enemy? Is he going to betray me? Does he truly love me?

The Shadow

The monster under the bed. Repressed feelings. Deep trauma. Festering guilt. These all possess the dark energy of the shadow. This is the dark force of the unexpressed, unrealized, rejected, feared aspects of the hero and represented by the main antagonist or villain.

The shadow challenges the hero in ways far more powerful than the threshold guardian. Voldemort in the *Harry Potter* series; Darth Vader in *Star Wars*; the aliens in *War of the Worlds*. These are all shadows and **worthy opponents** for the hero, bringing out the best in her and usually demanding the ultimate in self-sacrifice (the hero's destiny).

The shadow is a mask worn by any number of archetype characters. Vogler gives the example of the drill sergeant played by Louis Gossett, Jr., in *An Officer and a Gentleman*; who wore the masks of both Mentor and Shadow. The shadow force, if internalized by the hero, may serve as a threshold guardian, to overcome; ultimately challenging the hero to overcome her greatest weakness and prevail.

The Trickster

Practically every Shakespearian play contains a jester or fool, who not only serves as comic relief but as **commentator**. This is because tricksters are usually witty and clever, even when ridiculous. Most successful comedians touch upon the pulse of a culture by offering commentary that is truism (often in the form of entertaining sarcasm).

References

Cameron, Julia. 1992. *The Artist's Way: a Spiritual Path to Higher Creativity*. Penguin Putnam. 222pp.

Campbell, Joseph. 1970. *The Hero with a Thousand Faces*. World Publishing Co. New York. 464pp.

Dillard, Annie. 1975. *Pilgrim at Tinker Creek*. Bantam Books. New York. 290pp.

Eisler, Riane. 1987. *The Chalice & the Blade*. Harper & Row. New York. 261pp.

Estes, Clarissa Pinkola. 1995. *Women Who Run with the Wolves*. Ballantine Books. New York. 537pp.

Henderson, Mary. 1997. *Star Wars: The Magic of Myth*. Bantam Spectra. New York. 214pp.

Murdock, Maureen. 1988. *The Woman's Dictionary of Myth and Symbols*. Harper and Row. San Francisco.

Murdock, Maureen. 1990. *The Heroine's Journey: Woman's Quest for Wholeness*. Shambhala Publications, Inc., Boston.

Pearson, Carol S. 1991. *Awakening the Heroes Within*. *Harper*. San Francisco.

Pearson, Carol S. 1998. *The Hero Within: Six Archetypes We Live By*. Harper. San Francisco. 3rd Edition.

Pearson, Ridley. 2007. "Getting Your Act(s) Together". In: *Writer's Digest*. April, 2007.

Stone, Merlin. 1978. *When God Was a Woman*. Harvest Books. 320pp.

Vogler, Christopher. 1998. *The Writer's Journey: Mythic Structure for Writers*. 2nd Edition. Michael Wiese Productions, Studio City, California. 326pp.

K. ● Write About What You Know

How many times have you been told to write about what you know? And how many times have you trusted that advice? Well, how interesting is that?!? We think our lives are dull, boring, and mundane. We write to get away from it, don't we?

Well, yes...and no...

In the final analysis, even good "escapist" writing, like some science fiction, despite its alien settings and creatures of imagination, is grounded in the realities of our every-day lives, which form the basis of human nature. Love, ambition, trust, hate, envy, honor, courage. All these are universal human traits which the writer is tapping into and ultimately is writing about.

"In the 19th-century, John Keats wrote to a nightingale, an urn, a season. Simple, everyday things that he knew," say Kim Addonizio and Dorianne Laux in *The Writer's Guide to Creativity*. "Walt Whitman described the stars, a live oak, a field...They began with what they knew, what was at hand, what shimmered around them in the ordinary world."

The advice, "write what you know" isn't about literal truths; it's about what you know inside. As

SF author Marg Gilks says, "You know more than you think."

Twisted Truths & Inner Knowledge

In an article in *Writing World*, Gilks discusses how a writer can use her own knowledge and experiences in everyday life and translate them into something far from ordinary. You start with universal experiences.

Get Emotional

What excites you; what frightens you; what angers you, makes you sad, happy. These are emotions we all feel. When we give our characters experiences similar to our own, we breathe life into both character and experience and provide the reader an anchor for her heart.

Get Sensational

You know how it feels when the sun shines on your face or the rain drenches you. You know how it feels to have your knees shake with fatigue after a long climb on a hot day or the invigorating freshness of a cool lake in summer.

Get People Around You

My neighbor has a funny way of focusing his gaze slightly off me when he talks, as if he can't look me directly in the eyes. When the paperboy approaches my house to deliver the paper, he strides with a lilting gait as he listens to hip-hop on his iPod.

Drawing from what you observe and know of the people around you is one of a writer's most treasured resources for character description. I always carry a notebook with me no matter where I go, even if it's only to the grocery store (see Chapter W).

I Came, I Saw, I Researched

Of course, you *know* I was going to say it: doing research is another way of "knowing" something. Once you have done the research, you certainly know about a subject, provided you've done a good enough job.

What you might not have realized is that a writer is potentially always doing research; whether you're on the bus going to a movie downtown, taking a course at the community college or simply having a discussion with a friend. You are a student of life; that's what an artist is.

Many premises and ideas, particularly in the science fiction genre (but certainly not confined to this genre) need to be supported by careful research if you are going to pull them off. This is also what they mean when they say "write what you know". What they're saying is—okay, what *I'm* saying—is: you can write about *anything*, provided you either already have or gain sufficient knowledge about the subject. What was once esoteric pursuit has become easily accessed information through online resources. Of course, the down side to this is that you must be careful to ensure that your sources are accurate and reliable. The Internet is...well...the Internet. I give more details on this in Chapter W.

Diana Gabaldon didn't live in 19th-century Scotland. Yet, her extensive research of that era enabled her to transport her characters and readers to a time she had never experienced. She accomplished this using a combination of acquired knowledge through re-search and inner knowledge of emotions and experiences.

Examples abound of writers who tapped into their hobby, day job or major interest. This is because of two things: 1) they are writing about something they know very well, but more importantly, 2) they are writing about something they are passionate about (see Chapter Z).

John Grisham was a trial lawyer when he wrote *The Firm*, which became a bestseller. His knowledge of jargon and procedures lent an element of gritty reality to his story but it was his "experience" in that realm that made the story sizzle with life. In my own books, I've drawn on my background as a scientist and field ecologist. I've made extensive use of my ecological expertise in world-building for my books.

The Magic of Storytelling

A writer is like a magician. You play upon what readers all "know" then surprise them with the unexpected.

Unleashing your imagination and letting it soar while grounding yourself in the realities of universal truths is the stuff of which stories are made. This is what most of us mean when we say "write what you know."

"Unless you are writing about a personal tragedy," says Tina Morgan of *Fiction Factor*, "you will have to use your imagination. Use the creativity that drives you to write in the first place. Take those feelings you have every day and amplify them. Make them more intense, more vivid. Before you know it, you will be 'writing what you know'."

"Next time you hear 'write what you know,' " says Gilks, "you'll realize that you know an awful lot about what matters most in a story's success. It's waiting only to be shaped by your imagination."

Write Real

Literary Agent Rachelle Gardner provided a great definition of "write what you know" on her blog. Here's an excerpt:

> Most people think "write what you know" means you have to put characters in situations you're personally familiar with. If you're a mom with five kids, you should write a mom story. If you've fought cancer and won, you should write

about that. But in my opinion, that's not what it means.

Write what you know means write with *authenticity* about thoughts, feelings, experiences of life. Be honest. Write from a deep place. Don't write from the surface. Whether you're writing about parenthood or cancer or anything else... be real.

Don't reflect what you know from other people or the media... write what you know from your own inner life.

References

Addonizio, Kim and Dorianne Laux. 1999. "Sweat the Small Stuff." In: *The Writer's Guide to Creativity*. Writer's Digest, Cincinnati, Ohio.

Gardner, Rachelle. 2008. "Write What You Know". In: *Rants & Ramblings, On Life as a Literary Agent*. http://cba-ramblings.blogspot.com/2008/07/write-what-you-know.html

Gilks, Marg. 2001. "Write What You Know: You know more than you think". In: *Writing World*. http://www.writing-world.com/fiction/know.shtml

Morgan, Tina. 2001. "Write What You Know". In: *Fiction Factor, the Online Magazine for Fiction Writers*. http://www.fictionfactor.com/articles/whatyouknow.html

105

L. ● Long Form, Short Form

*I didn't have time to write a short letter,
so I wrote a long one instead*
—Blaise Pascal

Figuring out what you are writing isn't always as easy as you think. Many of us when we begin a story may think we are writing a short story when we are actually writing a novel; or vice versa. I had several editors of magazines tell me just that: "This feels more like a novel than a short story" they said—and rejected it. So, what are you really writing? Or, more to the point, what *should* you be writing?

Jack Bickham, author of *Elements of Fiction Writing: Scene and Structure*, tells us that, "story length, author intention, traditional expectations of the audience, and all sorts of things may affect the form a story may take." He goes on to explain that "the short story writer is taught that a short story has a 'beginning, middle and end' or perhaps 'a situation, a complication, a climax and a denouement.' The novelist may hear advice such as 'paint a broader picture' or 'give the characters more depth' or even 'make all your chapters twenty pages long'—none of it very darned helpful." Bickham is talking about the difference between "structure"—which is the internal 'guts' of every story—and "form", which is how it's told (see also Chapter A).

How we choose to tell a story (e.g., length, setting, POV, etc.) depends on what the story is about and what we want to focus on.

Defining Story Length & Terminology

Let's start out with defining what you are writing by length. The forms, as defined by the *Science Fiction & Fantasy Writers of America* appear in Table 1.

Table 1: Terminology for Story Lengths

Name	Description
Drabble (Flash Fiction)	Exactly 100 words
Flash Fiction	Less than 500 words
Short short Fiction	500-1,000 words
Short Story	Less than 7,500 words
Novelette	7,500 to 17,500 words
Novella	17,500 to 40,000 words
Novel	More than 40,000 words

There are variations on these demarcations, depending on the source; however, they are all close to those given above. The novelette and novella are apparently being passed over in favor of the shorter novel and longer short story. In the science fiction genre, however, they are still going strong and provide an excellent venue for the beginning writer wishing to venture into writing a novel. Many science fiction authors went this route. Nancy Kress and Ray Bradbury are two that come to mind. Both were consummate short story and novella writers before venturing into the arena of the novel.

While short stories normally range from 1,000 to 7,500 words, those less than 5,000 are easier to market because they are more easily placed by the publication.

Vignettes & Chapters

Although a vignette is customarily under 1,000 words, it really has nothing to do with word count, because it is based on theme. A vignette provides new insight into a character or the relationship between two or more characters.

Chapters have no impact on how your story is classified by word count. A story with less than 7,000 words will still be classified as a short story, even if it has chapters. There are no standard criteria for chapters, whose lengths vary widely among novels from one page to over twenty pages. Theme, plot, POV format, scene type, etc., along with personal preference of the writer, all determine length of a chapter.

Short Vs. Long—What's Your Focus?

A short story only has 5,000 words to get your story across while a novel has over ten times that many words to do the same. It 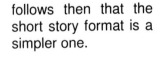 follows then that the short story format is a simpler one.

Novels provide a sense of change, growth and solutions to problems and conflicts. Short stories must be more succinct, contain fewer characters and subplots, have less complicated story arcs and a single theme. A short story is a poem to a novel's prose. A short story is a statement to a novel's argument.

"If the novel is a landscape, the short story is a close-up," says Shelley Lowenkopf in a short story workshop entitled *Telling Tales*. Lowenkopf adds, "The short story is an event, a moment in time, captured as if by accident."

"The short story doesn't have the luxury of depicting change; the closest it can come is awareness," Lowenkopf says. A short story, more than a novel, has the power to transport, disturb and enlighten.

Renowned short story authors like Edgar Allen Poe, Nathaniel Hawthorne and Somerset Maugham emphasize the importance of striving for one effect when writing a short story: the single effect you wish to leave with the reader at the end. This is accomplished by selecting events or situations that build quickly into a combustible response.

Pick Your Length: A Checklist

So, are you writing a short story or a novel? Which form best suits the story you are telling? Here's a short checklist to figure it out:

- ☐ does your story have several main characters and minor characters?
- ☐ is your story full of subplots?
- ☐ does your story contain multilayered

themes and story arcs?

☐ do your characters learn and change notably?

☐ is there significant change in your story?

☐ does your story contain several settings and sub-stories?

☐ does your story explore several ideas as opposed to one main idea?

☐ does your story investigate several issues rather than making a single point?

If you answered "yes" to more than three of the above, then no matter what you tell yourself you're writing, you are actually *thinking* "novel" and should do yourself a favor by writing one.

References

Bickham, Jack. 1993. *Elements of Fiction Writing: Scene and Structure.* Writer's Digest Books. Cincinnati, Ohio. 163pp.

Lowenkopf, Shelley. 2007. "Telling Tales". In: *The Portable Writer's Conference: Your Guide to Getting Published.* Quill Driver Books.

M. ● Master the Metaphor & Other Things

All the world's a stage
—William Shakespeare, *As You Like It*

During a brainstorming session, my business partner quizzed me on the major problems that writers face: "What are their Waterloos?" She was using metaphor to make a point. You don't have to look very far to find examples; everyday speech is full of them: like "raining cats and dogs; "table leg"; and "old flame".

Ray Bradbury once told me at a writers' conference that *story is metaphor*.

What's a Metaphor Anyway?

The word metaphor has its roots in the Greek word *metaphora* which means "transfer". In literature, a metaphor brings together dissimilar words to suggest similarity. Shakespeare in the above quote is comparing the world to a stage. Metaphor directly compares seemingly unrelated subjects as being or equal to each other. It is, therefore, considered more powerful than an analogy, which may acknowledge differences. Other rhetorical devices that involve comparison include *metonymy, synecdoche, simile, allegory* and *parable*. While these share common attributes with metaphor, each compares in a

111

different way.

What ARE Those Other Things?

Allegory is an extended metaphor in which an object, person or action is equated with the meaning that lies outside the narrative. In other words, allegory has both a literal and a representative meaning. Allegories can describe political or historical events and people or they can represent ideas. George Orwell's *Animal Farm* is a modern example of the first type, which describes the development of Russian communism through a revolt by farm animals. The allegory of ideas is common in medieval literature, as in Dante's *Divine Comedy*, in which the pilgrim, the common person, seeks salvation that is both helped and hindered by his reliance upon Reason (in the person of Virgil).

Fables and **parables** are types of allegory. A parable is also an extended metaphor, told as an anecdote to teach a moral lesson.

A **simile** uses words such as "like" or "as" to compare two ideas (e.g., as precise as a surgeon). Similes and metaphors both compare. Similes allow the two ideas to remain distinct in spite of their similarities, whereas metaphors equate two ideas despite their differences:

> **Simile**: His love was like a slow dance
>
> **Metaphor**: Love danced in her heart

Similes can imply comparison (e.g., His mind is like a sword) or be explicit (e.g., His mind is sharp like a sword). This is what makes the simile such a useful tool to the writer: you can choose to be vague, letting the reader infer the relationship, or be direct. Simile can also convey irony by using wry humor to play against expectations (e.g., as soft as a cactus; as quiet as a hungry two-year-old) or by subverting the stereotype (e.g., as precise as a *drunk* surgeon).

The term **synecdoche** substitutes a part for a whole or a whole for a part (e.g., the expression "all hands on deck" refers to the men; or the  expression "use your head" refers to your brain). Synecdoche is a common way to emphasize an important aspect of a character. For instance, a character might be described by a single body part, such as the eyes, which come to represent that character. The use of a specific item to describe all similar items is synecdoche (e.g., "could you pass the Kleenex?" referring to tissue paper) as is the use of the material to describe the object (e.g., "she's wearing some cool threads" refers to her entire outfit).

Metonymy uses one word to describe and represent another (e.g. the suits from Wall Street). Metonymy works by association whereas metaphor works through similarity.

113

Here's an example from Dirvin (1966) on the use of the word "fishing".

Metonymy: "fishing for pearls" draws from the idea of taking things from the ocean

Metaphor: "fishing for information" transfers the concept of fishing without a connection to the actual concept of taking "fish" out of the ocean.

Personification gives an idea, object or animal the qualities of a person (e.g., the darkness embraced her; the creek babbled over the rocks).

Types of Metaphor

On *Literaryzone*, Shruti Chandra Gupta (2008) tells us that there are at least eighteen different types of metaphor. Here are some of the coolest ones:

- **Extended metaphor** (also called telescoping metaphor): this is when details are added to the original metaphor (e.g., *All the world's a stage and men and women merely players*).

- An **implied metaphor** is an indirect metaphor where an implication to the whole is made (e.g., "shut your trap."). Mouth is implied through trap.

- A **dead metaphor** is just that: dead. Cliché (e.g., crown of glory). In a dead metaphor, the sense of a transferred image isn't present (e.g., to grasp a concept). By contrast, an **active metaphor** is new, not part of daily language and therefore noticeable (e.g., her blinking love). Gupta describes a **dormant metaphor** as when the meaning of a metaphor becomes unclear because it has become truncated (e.g., he was blazing).

- In a **submerged metaphor** the vehicle is implied, or indicated by one aspect (e.g., my winged thought). Here, the audience must supply the image of the bird.

- A **conceptual metaphor** has several metaphoric meanings in it to create a novel thought of universal concept. The conceptual metaphor mounts one identification on another (That throws some light on the question). Throwing light is a metaphor and there is no actual light.

Okay, so that wasn't eighteen; you get the picture (I guess that's another metaphor... Or is it metonymy?). Now that you have all the terminology, let's talk about using it.

Why Use Metaphor?

The Owl Online Writing Lab at Purdue University suggests why:

- **Metaphors enliven ordinary language:** creative writers have the power to make the ordinary strange and the strange ordinary, making life interesting again.

- **They encourage interpretation**: by their very nature, metaphors describe a deeper indirect truth rather than a literal truth, which invites the reader to think.

- **They give maximum meaning with a minimum of words**: when you write "John's office was a prison" you are suggesting a lot about how John felt at work (e.g., that he felt as if he was placed in solitary, in a cramped space, etc) that could take several paragraphs.

- **They create new meanings**: by letting you write about feelings, thoughts, and experiences for which there are no easy words.

- **They are a sign of genius**: "[T]he greatest thing by far is to be a master of metaphor." It is "a sign of genius, since a good metaphor implies an intuitive perception of the similarity in dissimilars." (Aristotle).

Metaphor Danger & Overload

Steve Almond warns us of the dangers of metaphors. "In the wrong hands [metaphors] become an assertion of the author's talents, rather than an effort to immerse us in the world of his characters," he says and adds, "They actually serve the purpose of distracting us, however charmingly, from the business at hand." An overextended or misused metaphor is often a sign of insecurity. Novice writers often fall into this trap. Remember the adage "less is more." Metaphors, Almond reminds us, may also distract readers from the most important words in the writer's arsenal—verbs.

The kinds of metaphor you use (extended metaphors particularly) rely a great deal on your  narrative voice, the type of story you're telling, and the language you're using. For instance, elaborate use of metaphor fits better in the rich narrative style of epic fantasy than in a contemporary thriller.

So, what is metaphor overload and how do you avoid it? Here's an example:

> John strode into the aft deck and saw Aeryn and Crais embracing. He stopped, heart slamming like the staccato percussion of a demon frag cannon on his wounded soul.

If you eliminate the simile here's what you get:

> John strode into the aft deck and saw Aeryn and Crais embracing. He stopped, heart slamming.

Removal of the simile activates the verb and focuses the reader's attention on John's visceral reaction. Which is more powerful?

If the verb is powerful enough, it eliminates the need for any additional modifier. Metaphor becomes redundant. "Heart slamming" already connotes the metaphor of percussive action.

Almond recommends that you do the following to avoid metaphor overload:

1. Review your verbs and make them active and as powerful as you can; then review your metaphor and its utility—if it's redundant, nix it.

2. "Interrogate" your metaphors about their comparative role—is the image of the comparison really what you wish to convey? By directing readers away from the literal truth, how are you redirecting them to the deeper truths of your piece?

Some Cool Examples

Here are two from Raymond Chandler's *The Long Goodbye*:

His hair was bone white.
I got the drunk up [the stairs] somehow. He was eager to help but his legs were rubber.

The metaphor is often tied in to the overall theme or plotline of the story, providing tone to the story and sometimes foreshadowing.

Exercise:

4. Compare a character to the following: a peacock; a sloth; a dung beetle; a rabbit. What physical and emotional connotations do you get?

5. Sarah's voice _____ like _____. Fill in the blanks based on these different potential relationships Sarah has to the POV character: a) his lover; b) his uptight arrogant boss; c) his cheating wife

6. Take a piece of your own writing and find all the metaphors and similes. Highlight them then interrogate them. What purpose are they fulfilling? Are they necessary?

References

Dirvin, René. 1966. *Conversion as a Conceptual Metonymy of Basic Event Schemata.*

Gupta, Shruti Chandra. 2007. Eighteen Types of Metaphor. In: Literaryzone. http://literaryzone.com/?p=99.

Kopp, Bryan M. 1998. "Using Metaphors in Creative Writing". In: *OWL Online Writing Lab at Perdue University.* http://owl.english.purdue.edu/handouts/print/general/gl_metaphor

119

N. ● Now It's Time for Revision!

You thought you were done once you sorted out the sluggish middle or figured out a great ending for your epic fantasy. Completing that first draft is just the beginning of a process to get your story published. Roll up your sleeves and get ready.

It's time for **Revision**. No piece of writing is complete without submitting to the scrutiny of the revision process.

In an article in *Writer's Digest* (February, 2008) Jordan E. Rosenfeld tells the story of what a student of hers said about revision. It's "like beating up a good friend. Now, why would I want to do that?" Because, says Rosenfeld, without a little pummeling all you have is a nice draft. She adds that in order for a novel these days to enter the competitive world of publishing, it needs the pummeled polish of revision.

Ten Ways to Revise Your Story

Rosenfeld provides ten things you should consider when revising your first (and subsequent) draft(s).

1. **Let your work breathe**: once you've completed your draft, set it aside for a

while. This lets you make objective observations about your writing when you return.

2. **Dig deep**: now that you have the whole story before you, you can restructure plotlines, subplots, events and characters to best reflect your overall story. Don't be afraid to remove large sections; you will likely add others. You may also merge two characters into one or add a character or change a character's gender or age.

3. **Take Inventory**: it's good to take stock of how each chapter contributes to plotline and theme; root out the inconsistencies as you relate the minutiae to the whole.

4. **Highlight the Surges**: some passages will stand out as being particularly stunning; pay attention to them in each chapter and apply their energy to the rest of your writing.

5. **Purge & Unclutter**: make a point of shortening everything; this forces you to use more succinct language, replacing adjectives and adverbs with power-verbs. Lik-  en it to writing for a magazine with only so much space (check out Chapter U for more ideas). Doing this will tighten prose and make it more clear. Reading aloud,

particularly dialogue, can help streamline your prose.

6. **Point of view**: this is the time to take stock of whether you've chosen the best point of view for the story (see Chapter P). You may wish to experiment with different points of view at this stage and the results may surprise you.

7. **Make a plot promise**: given that you are essentially making a promise to your readers, it is advisable that you revisit that promise. Tie up your plot points; don't leave any hanging unless you're intentionally doing this, but be aware that readers don't generally like it. Similarly, if you've written a scene that is lyrical, beautiful and compelling but doesn't contribute to your plotline, nix it. But keep it for another story; chances are, it will work elsewhere. The trick is to file it where you can later find it.

8. **Deepen your characters**: the revision process is an ideal time to add subtle detail to your main characters. A nervous scratch of his beard, an absent twisting of the ring on her finger, the frequent use of a particular expression: all these can be worked in throughout the story, in your later drafts. Even minor characters can shine and be unique. When you paint your minor characters with more detail, you create a more three-dimensional tapestry for your main characters to walk through. This heightens realism in your

story and involvement of your reader.

9. **Write scenes**: use the revision process to convert flat narrative into "scene" through dramatization. Narrative summaries read like lecture or polemic. They tend to be passive, slow, and less engaging. Scenes include action, tension and conflict, dialogue and physical movement.

10. **Be concrete**: Rosenfeld describes your novel as a world in which your reader enters and wants to stay in for a while. You make it easy for her by adding concrete details for her to envision and relate to. Ground your characters in vivid setting, rich but unobtrusive detail. Don't abandon them to a generic and prosaic setting, drinking "beverages" and driving "vehicles" on "roads"; instead brighten up their lives by having them speeding along Highway 66 in a Mini Cooper, while sipping a Pinot Noir.

Here are a few other things you can do:

1. **Proof read backwards.** Because many writers are bad spellers (go figure), chances are you will have spelling errors that even the computer spell-check won't catch (see Chapter X), such as homonym errors. Every writer has his or her own particular variety of typo that we often subconsciously "correct" during the edit phase. Reading your script backwards helps you to see it differently and per-

haps break out of the subconscious correcting mode.

2. **Check for overly long sentences.** Set a sentence length threshold, say twenty words maximum. Scrutinize these for alteration. You can break a long sentence into two sentences or you can remove excessive phrases or modifiers. Short sentences read better than long ones.

Every serious writer owns a copy of Strunk and White's *The Elements of Style*. I recommend that you also keep a dictionary (preferably less than ten years old but more than two pounds in weight) on hand as you revise. You may also find grammar handbooks a good tool to use when revising (again, see Chapter X).

Ruthless Revision, Kind Pace...

Remember to pace yourself when revising; otherwise you may become overwhelmed and discouraged, even confused into incessant rewrites (see below). Your story needs to settle between revision stages.

As Rosenfeld says, "you don't have to beat up your good friend all at once." He suggests going through your novel looking for one aspect to address at a time. This is also a more efficient way to address any aspect you are dealing with. Of course, that translates into multiple trips through your story, but it's worthwhile. You've designed the car; now you're the mechanic, doing the final finishing touches to prepare it for its journey on the road. Take your time and give your baby the attention it deserves in this critical stage.

When Do You Know You're Finished?

A student of mine once asked me how many drafts it took to get the final version of a story. I answered cagily: as many as you need. I wasn't trying to be cheeky or elusive. In truth, this is a question that only you can answer; and it will be different with each story you write.

To the question "when do you know you're finished?" Robert J. Sawyer replied "when you've taken out all the boring bits."

George Lucas once said in an interview about the remaking of the first Star Wars Trilogy that in the film industry, projects were never finished; only abandoned. What he meant by this was that at some point in the creative and revision process of polishing a story, you have to stop and show it to the world. Let your baby walk and stand on its own.

This is a big step for all beginning writers and many freeze. Terrified at the idea of failure or censure, they end up sabotaging their own work. If you're emotionally or psychologically not ready for the consequences of getting published (see

Chapter Z), then you will falter, procrastinate, forever fuss over your creation and convince yourself that it isn't ready. In truth, it's *you* who aren't ready.

This is a shame because to have written an entire novel is a great accomplishment. You've already done what over 80% of those who embark on a book don't do: finish. To halt the process by entering into a perpetual cycle of revision is admitting defeat when you have really won the major battle. It's like that fatal stumble on the last leg of a homerun.

If the idea is to publish, then you need to give yourself a kind of deadline or goal, based on something that makes sense to you and is realistically achievable:

- I will stop editing this story and send it out by such and such a date
- I will revise this story until I get it to so many pages, etc.

It really doesn't matter what that goalpost is, so long as you adhere to it. Below is a brief checklist on what to look for to convince yourself that you are ready to send out that baby:

Revision Checklist

☐ Did you set your manuscript aside to let it breathe a little before starting the revision process?

☐ Did you remove all the boring bits?

126

- ☐ Does it read clean (have you removed extraneous parts that don't move the plot and keep your story fluid)?

- ☐ Does the ending reflect the story promise at the beginning and provide a good resolution?

- ☐ Did you tie up the subplots and do they make sense?

- ☐ Did you do a thorough copy edit, spell-check and grammar-check?

- ☐ Do you have a great hook in the beginning?

- ☐ Did you write a synopsis that reflects your book and does it kick ass? (Because if it doesn't it may reflect a less than exciting novel)

- ☐ Have you found a publishing house that you think is a good fit with your story? (I.e., they publish similar things)

- ☐ Have you spent at least as much time polishing your query letter and synopsis as you did on any other aspect of your story?

If your answer is **yes** to all of the above, you no longer have an excuse; send it out.

Remember that no work of art is perfect; mainly because that is impossible to define in art, given that it is different things to different people (I recommend reading *A Portrait of an Artist as a Young Man* by James Joyce). A piece may be wrong for one market but just right for another.

Second Chances?

Various authors have had the opportunity to revise a story after it was published, either due to a reprinting or a re-issuing in a new format. Some do, but many don't. I recall the foreward that Aldous Huxley wrote in 1946 to his classic book, *Brave New World*, originally published in 1932:

> *To pore over the literary shortcomings of twenty years ago, to attempt to patch a faulty work into the perfection it missed at its first execution, to spend one's middle age in trying to mend the artistic sins committed and bequeathed by that different person who was oneself in youth—all this is surely vain and futile. And that is why this new Brave New World is the same as the old one. Its defects as a work of art are considerable; but in order to correct them I should have to rewrite the book—and in the process of rewriting, as an older, other person, I should probably get rid not only of some of the faults of the story, but also of such merits as it originally possessed. And so, resisting the temptation to wallow in artistic remorse, I prefer to leave both well and ill alone and to think about something else.*

Art is self-expression; expression is a reflection of the culture and time in which you live. Stories are a snapshot of time and place. Treat your art like life; some revision is good but at some point you need to just LIVE.

References

Huxley, Aldous. 1946. Forward. In: *Brave New World*. Penguin Books. Middlesex, England. 7-14pp.

Joyce, James. 1916. *A Portrait of the Artist as a Young Man*. Penguin. 384pp.

Rosenfeld, Jordan E. 2008. "Novel Revision for the Faint of Heart". In: *Writer's Digest*. February, 2008.

Sawyer, Robert J. 2008. SF Writer Website: http://www.sfwriter.com.

Strunk, William Jr. and E.B. White. 1979. Elements of Style. McMillan Publishing Co., Inc. New York. 85pp.

O. ● Outline or Synopsis ...And Why Bother?

Talent isn't enough. You need motivation—and persistence too: what Steinbeck called a blend of faith and arrogance. When you're young, plain old poverty can be enough, along with an insatiable hunger for recognition. You have to have that feeling of "I'll show them." If you don't have it don't become a writer. It's part animal, it's primitive, but if you don't want to rise above the crowd, forget it.
—Leon Uris

When I was just beginning as a writer, the publisher guideline request "submit a synopsis and sample chapters" struck fear into my heart. There was something terrifyingly daunting about writing and sending a succinct compelling summary of my novel packaged in just a few pages. As author Katherine Eliska Kimbriel said, "The instinctive response [of the author] is to clap on a helmet and start digging a trench." I had a right to be terrified. In some ways the synopsis is the hardest thing for a novelist to write. Yet it is the first thing most publishers and agents want (and have time) to see of your cherished project (aside from those sample chapters, of course). Every fiction writer who wants to sell in the current market must know how to write a synopsis because that's what an editor wants to see first. Most editors (if they're good) are overworked with little enough time to answer their phones, much less their mail.

I'm not going to describe at length how to write a synopsis here. If you want to see an excellent summary of what a good synopsis should look like, take a look at Tricia Ares's excellent post in the Modern Matriarch. There are many excellent descriptions by professional editors, agents and other writers who describe what a synopsis is and even give examples (see some of them in my reference section below). And I do give you a short summary of their main points under the HOW Section below. But I suggest you go to my reference section below and look them up.

What I'd like to do first is give you some very good reasons WHY you should write that dreaded synopsis, and way before you finish your book.

Why Bother?

First of all, I'd like to dispel some common misconceptions about synopses:

A synopsis is NOT an outline. Both are useful to the writer, yet each serves a very different purpose. An outline is a tool (usually just for the writer) that sketches plot items of a book. It provides a skeleton or framework of plot, people, places and their relationships to the storyline. It

131

permits the writer to ultimately gauge scene, set-ing, and character depth or even determine whether a character is required (every character must have a reason to be in the book, usually to move the plot). For writers just beginning, this is an excellent tool to keep the narrative spare and compelling and to remove superfluous characters and scenes (a common inclination for beginning writers). A synopsis, on the other hand, is an in-depth summary of the entire book that weaves thematic elements with plot to portray a compelling often multi-level story arc. This is usually what an editor wants to see, although I have seen them request an outline as well. To put it basically, the outline describes what happens when and to whom, while the synopsis includes why.

There is no such thing as a "Killer Synopsis"; a synopsis so good it will sell the book outright. However, stories of such "fairy-tale" occurrences do continue to abound. I know of one about a fantasy writer who supposedly landed an agent then a three-book deal for her first trilogy with a large publishing house on the basis of a cover letter and such a synopsis. This just isn't so. Other factors were in play here; like the myth of an overnight success (in which the author's hard work in areas related are somehow overlooked). No publisher chooses to buy a book on the basis of a synopsis only. Such an event could only result from a combination of serendipitous fac-tors, one of the most important being timing (luck) and what an editor is currently looking for in an imprint.

"Killer synopsis" aside, what a synopsis does

(along with the sample chapters and extremely important query or cover letter; see Chapter Q) is get your manuscript read by an editor. That's the real purpose of a synopsis. It's essentially part of your sales pitch. Think of it as a detailed version of the back book jacket. An editor makes his/her decision to look at your manuscript based on these three items:

- Query/cover letter (intro to you)
- sample chapters
- synopsis

And, remember that, ultimately, their decision resides with whether your project fits their own imprint at the time.

If that isn't reason enough to write a synopsis of your novel, here are two others:

- A synopsis of your novel goes beyond the outline to help polish elements of and answer questions perplexing you on story arc, characterization, plot and setting. It helps you weave your novel's elements into a well-integrated story that is compelling at many levels. For this reason, it makes sense to write drafts of your synopsis as you go along in the novel. That way it's useful to both you and to the editor and then it's more or less written when you need to submit it along with sample chapters...and not quite as daunting a task either.

- Lastly, your synopsis is often used internally by the publishing house staff (by artist, copywriter and sales department) once your novel has been accepted. Parts of it often end up on the back book jacket along with those important testimonials.

So get going on it now. Don't wait. Make the synopsis work for you throughout your novel's journey.

What's in a Synopsis?

Elizabeth Lyon, author of *The Sell Your Novel Toolkit*, suggests that a synopsis should usually include these seven items:

- Theme
- Setting and Period
- Plot summary
- Character sketches
- Dialogue
- Emotional turning points
- Subplots

The **theme**, explains Lyons, "provides a rudder for an entire novel." She suggests condensing it into one sentence or phrase: to have a friend you must be a friend; cooperation lies at the heart of evolution; love is the true source of human wealth; there's no place like home. You can also portray your theme in a single word (e.g., forgiveness, revenge, trust, prejudice, evolution). Note that these differ from narrative description that focuses on plot items such as "David goes

to war" or "Dorothy runs away from home."
You can provide **setting and period** in one or two short sentences. One way to accomplish this is to incorporate setting and period with the hook of the synopsis. In the synopsis I wrote for *The Last Summoner*, that is what I did:

> *On June 14th 1410 in Grunwald, Prussia, one of medieval history's most decisive battles is about to destroy the powerful Teutonic Order, slaughtering virtually all its monk knights. How would history have changed if this arrogant Nazi-like order had not underestimated its enemy and had instead won to continue sweeping through north-east Europe, unscathed, in its ambitious crusade for Christendom? One girl will decide which way the battle goes.*

Lyon suggests that the **plot summary** is like a skeleton upon which to flesh out character and theme. Two things you need to consider are that 1) you must summarize the complete novel (beginning, middle and end) and 2) you should not confuse a plot summary (essentially an outline) with a synopsis, which incorporates more than plot.

"The best-written and most impressive synopses," says Lyon, "are those that make it clear that a story is character driven." Lyon recommends that you limit your sketches to the main characters that drive principle theme in the story. The first sentence of my synopsis of *Collision with Paradise* focuses on the main character:

When Genevieve Dubois, Zeta Corp's hot shot starship pilot accepts a research mission aboard ZAC I to the mysterious planet Eos, she not only collides with her guilty past but with her own ultimate fantasy.

While the sentence conveys information about the plot, it is given from the viewpoint of a character's motivations and feelings. The reader is informed at the outset that character development is at the heart of the story.

You may use **dialogue** or quotes in a synopsis to great effect, so long as this is done sparingly and judiciously. Not only does this break up the page and make it more interesting, but it provides a direct sample of your work. I tend to use dialogue and quotes in most of my synopses. In my synopsis of *Collision with Paradise*, I inserted a quote from the novel to show the mood and beliefs of the protagonist, while revealing information.

We enter the story as *ZAC* [the sentient spaceship] nears the jungle planet of Eos, shrouded in mystery and enchanting myth. Described by some as Eden-like, its people appear as naked simpletons with no vices, yet they enjoy all the comforts of a superior though largely invisible bio-technology. Genevieve is awoken to do ship-systems verification, leaving the rest of the crew in hibe and fueling the ship. This suits Genevieve

just fine; she gets along better with
ZAC's quirky rather ribald personality
than she does with the rest of her
human crew and often seeks time alone
to think, like in the bow-side lounge,
peering out at the Pleiedes Nebula her
ship is sailing through:

*"Vapours of colour swirled around them
like an eerie yet fanciful dance, as
though the ship was drifting mindlessly
inside a huge spider's web. She took in
several deep breaths to keep from
gasping at the enormity of it all. If there
was a God, this was assuredly His
retreat, she thought with sudden
solemnity. It was too vast and
incomprehensible to be a home to
anyone else, much less any human...
But there probably was no God, she
decided. At least not a warm-hearted
one. How could such a God have
created such a cold and amorally
complex universe?... One that had taken
her husband and her sweet child and
given her nothing in return except
longing..."*

The **emotional turning points** are the focal
events that are directly linked to the theme of the
story. These are the "so what" parts of the story
plot—where the character reaches an epiphany
and, as a result, changes—and are ultimately
linked to the climax of the story.

137

You should be careful when including **subplots** in your synopsis. Obviously, you can't include them all. The ones that belong in the synopsis are those that most closely influence the path of theme, and most affect the main character. Subplots, like any exposition, must be seamlessly included.

Write it in Steps

Author Marg Gilks very wisely suggests not to let yourself be daunted by the enormity of the task. She advises to break the synopsis down and write it in steps:

STEP ONE—Writing the Outline: "Sit down to that final reading with a pen and paper beside you," says Marg. "As you finish reading each chapter, write down a one- or two-paragraph summary of what happened where and to which character." Marg asks you to observe any themes running through your chapters (if you don't already have them in your mind). Look for symbolism that your wise muse may have inadvertently slipped in there while you weren't paying attention. Take note of them. They'll come in handy later.

STEP TWO—Creating the Thematic Skeleton: After step one, you are essentially left with an outline; a useful device to refer to when you wish to rework the story, but lacking the essence of why the story is interesting and saleable. Step two involves a deeper analysis of character motivation linked with essential plot items that affect the characters.

To create the thematic skeleton, you need to select your most important characters, the ones who carry the plot and story arc (see Chapter C). The ones you care about. Then you need to decide what their major needs are, what their major weaknesses and obstacles are and how they will (or will not) overcome them. Once you have done this for each major character, you need to tie each into the major theme, often called the **overarching theme** or **arc**. Ultimately you should be striving to come up with a one-line story summary (the overarching theme usually), the kind of five-second response you would give to the inevitable question: "What's it about?" Reducing a book to a single line may seem difficult at first, but the more you analyze the thematic elements that run through your chapters, the more likely you are to come up with something. At any rate, now, you have a thematic skeleton.

STEP THREE—Putting Muscle on Bone. Now, write your skeleton into a story. Essentially, you are storytelling in the tradition of oral storytelling. Show enthusiasm. Entice. Provoke. Many writers who've struggled with synopses suggest you think of describing the story to a friend as though it was a movie you just saw and were trying to convince them to see. It is a pitch, after all. Others suggest that you imagine yourself writing a book jacket blurb for the novel (not a wasted pursuit, either, because ultimately the publisher wants you to write this!). You need to write this to incite the casual book browser's curiosity and urge him to buy your book. Go to your local bookstore or peruse books in your own library to get an idea.

Write the synopsis like a story, complete with hook, building to crisis and then climax and denouement. A great way to research effective hooks is to watch movie trailers, says Tricia Ares. "Hooks [usually] begin with the lead character, his/her crisis and how he/she intends to resolve it." Here's one written by Krista at IMDb for *The Golden Compass*:

> *It was no ordinary life for a young girl: living among scholars in the hallowed halls of Jordan College and tearing unsupervised through Oxford's motley streets on mad quests for adventure. But Lyra's greatest adventure would begin closer to home, the day she heard hushed talk of an extraordinary particle.*

"Avoid the use of adjectives and adverbs, and referencing your clever plot devices," says Ares. "Stick to the Action, Emotion and Motivation that move the story forward." AEM high, folks!

Synopses often start with the main character. Always keep in mind what is DIFFERENT about your book, what makes it stand out; this is likely why it will also be interesting to both the editor and the reader.

Oh, and lastly, that one or two line distillation of the book that you came up with can be included in the synopsis, but might be put to better use in your cover letter.

Housekeeping Details

I'm not going to give you many details on synopsis form and structure, partly because this varies greatly between different publishing houses, editors and agents. For instance, the length of a synopsis may vary from one page to twenty pages and its style will vary accordingly.

You're best to research and enquire. Most publishing houses and magazines give you this information in their submission guideline section. However, there are a few universal rules agreed upon by most publishers that can give you a head start. Here are some:

- Always write the synopsis in the present tense (the Budong eats Jarek; not the Budong ate Jarek).

- Write the synopsis from the author's perspective and use vivid language (use active power verbs, avoid modifiers).

- The first time you introduce a character in a synopsis, type the name in CAPITAL letters, but do this only the first time the character is mentioned. Stay consistent with how you refer to the character (use the same designation: not Jarek the first time and then Mr. Pook the second).

- Reveal the entire story in the synopsis, from beginning to the end, regardless of whether you included sample chapters—

don't leave out the ending!

I recommend Elizabeth Lyon's *The Sell Your Novel Toolkit*, which provides examples of different types of synopses of differing lengths and differing styles, with good commentary of why things did or didn't work.

Exercise:

5. Using the "every novel is a war" or "man versus society" model, list each character and who s/he is fighting and why (see Chapter P).

6. If relevant, chart the twelve steps of your story's "Hero's Journey" complete with each character archetype and why (see Chapter J).

7. Write a one-sentence premise and/or theme of your story and how your main character(s) will dramatize it (see Chapters P and C).

8. Write a ten-sentence back jacket blurb of your story then "pitch" it to a trusted friend.

References

Ares, Tricia. 2007. *The Synopsis: a Powerful Marketing Tool for Writers*. In: Modern Matriarch, http://modernmatriarch.wordpress.com/2007/08/24/the-synopsis.

Gilks, Marg. 2001. *How to Write a Synopsis*. In: Writing World, http://www.writing-world.com/publish/synopsis.

Lyon, Elizabeth. 2002. *The Sell Your Novel Tool Kit*. Revised Edition. Perigee Trade. 320pp.

Marshall, Evan. 1998. *The Marshall Plan for Novel Writing*. Cincinnati, Ohio. Writer's Digest.

P. ● Plotting with Purpose

What is Plot & Why is it so Important?

"The common definition of plot," says Ansen Dibell, author of *Elements of Fiction Writing: Plot*, "is that it's whatever happens in the story." But, "it doesn't tell you how to make one," he adds. "Plot is built of significant events in a given story—significant because they have important consequences."

"Plot is the things characters do, feel, think, or say, that make a difference to what comes afterward," says Dibell. I've also heard authors describe plot as all the nasty things they throw at their main character to stop them from getting where or what they want or need.

Plot is motion. "Plot is a verb," says Dibell.

If something—or someone—isn't moving, then your plot isn't going anywhere and it's not taking your reader anywhere either.

The first question Jack Hodgins asks about your plot in his *A Passion for Narrative* is:

Whose story is it? Whom do you care most about? Why?

Okay, that was really three questions. But they all relate to finding out who carries your main plot question and arc. Hodgins asks more questions like: 1) what's your main character's purpose or goal? 2) what's at stake? and 3) are there causal relationships between an event and the next?

What's at Stake?

"For a reader to care about your story, there has to be something at stake—something of value to gain, something of value to be lost," writes Dibell. Paul Boles, in his book *Storycrafting*, called it "wrestling".

Dibell uses the example of *Lord of the Flies* to explore this question further. What I like about this classic by William Golding is that what's at stake—survival itself—is a struggle at many levels. The obvious struggle is to live: after crash landing, a group of boys try to stay alive on an uninhabited tropical island. But the more subtle struggle is one's quality of life, through each boy's morality, ethics and compassion. The story explores the internal battle between fear and courage, distrust of the unknown and curiosity as played out by various characters.

"In other words," says Dibell, "there can be an outer plot and an inner one, which in some sense mirrors and reinforces it, or conflicts and contrasts with it."

Some Basic Plot Approaches

Although plots will vary as much as individual stories, there are some basic elements and forms. Here are some:

- **Cause and Effect**: this is simply when one event leads to another. Many writers talk about scenes and sequels when constructing stories (see below).

- **Thematic**: this is where events are tied together by a thematic thread, a common relationship, a central event, place, character or theme.

- **Lyric**: this is when plot is organized like music, with a cyclical return to key images, events or themes that grow deeper each time (*Finnegan's Wake*, by James Joyce, for example.)

- **Hero's Journey**: this plot approach follows the mythic steps of the hero's journey (see Chapter J).

When Nancy Kress, author of *Beggars in Spain*, held a workshop at a writers' conference in Vancouver recently, she described another plot approach called: "every novel is a war."

She had every writer in the workshop ask five questions: 1) who is at war? 2) who's fighting? 3) what are the battles? 4) who wins and who loses? 5) what did this war mean? The last question brings in theme, an important element to consider when deciding on plot elements.

Kress described some common and useful plot elements. Along with some of hers, I've provided a list below with examples from books and film:

- A stranger arrives (*Pride and Prejudice*)
- Quest/pursuit (*The Golden Compass*; *Contact*)
- Rescue/escape (*Jurassic Park*; *Romancing the Stone*)
- Rivalry (*The Prestige*)
- Oppression/dystopia (*Brave New World*; *1984*; *Fahrenheit 451*)
- Underdog/prejudice (*Beggars in Spain*; *Schindler's List*)
- Obstacles to Love (*The Go-between*; *The Illusionist*)
- Puzzle/mystery (*The DaVinci Code*)
- Sacrifice (*A Tale of Two Cities*)
- Ironic events/Redemption (*Atonement*)
- Adventure goes awry (*Deliverance*)
- World/natural disaster (*Day of the Triffids*)
- Fighting the monster/the "monster" within (*Lord of the Flies*; *The Matrix*)
- Humanity versus technology (*I, Robot*)
- Humanity evolves (*Darwin's Radio*)

Plot Structure—Scene to Sequel

According to Dwight Swain, author of *Tech-*

146

niques of the Selling Writer, stories progress in a series of "scenes" bridged by "sequels". This is essentially how plot moves forward, one step at a time; in this case one scene at a time. If you find yourself getting confused by scene and sequel," says author Melinda Goodin, "another way of thinking about the chain is as 'cause and effect', or 'action and reaction'."

Swain maps out story building by breaking down both scene and sequel this way:

A **Scene** has the following three-part pattern:

1. Goal
2. Conflict
3. Disaster

A **Sequel** has the following three-part pattern:

1. Reaction
2. Dilemma
3. Decision

Randy Ingermanson, publisher of a popular e-zine on writing fiction, describes the three elements of a powerful **scene** this way:

1. **Goal:** what your POV character wants at the beginning of the Scene. It must be specific and clear. The reason your POV character must have a Goal is that it makes your character proactive. Your character is not passively waiting for the universe to unfold. Your character is going after what she wants, just as your reader wishes she could do. Any character who wants something desper-

ately is an interesting character. Even if she's not nice, she's interesting.

2. **Conflict:** the series of obstacles your POV character faces on the way to reaching her Goal. You must have Conflict in your **Scene.** It's boring if your POV character reaches her Goal with no Conflict. Victory means nothing without a struggle. So make your POV character struggle and your reader will live out that struggle too.

3. **Disaster:** when your POV character fails to reach her Goal. Don't give her the Goal. Winning is boring! When a **Scene** ends in victory, your reader feels no reason to turn the page. Make something awful happen. Hang your POV character off a cliff and your reader will turn the page to see what happens next.

"The purpose of a **Sequel** is to follow the **Scene,**" says Ingermanson. "A **Scene** ends on a Disaster, and you can't immediately follow that up with a new **Scene,** which begins with a Goal. Why? Because when you've just been slugged with a serious setback, you can't just rush out and try something new. You've got to recover. That's basic psychology." Here are the steps of a sequel:

1. **Reaction:** the emotional consequence to a Disaster. When something awful happens, you stagger for awhile, off-balance. Show your POV character reacting viscerally to her Disaster. Show

148

her hurting. Give your reader a chance to hurt with your characters. This is not a time for action, it's a time for re-action. A time to weep. But you can't stagger around in pain forever. In real life, if people do that they lose their friends. In fiction, if you do it, you lose your readers. Eventually, your POV character needs to get a grip. To take stock. To look for options. And the problem is that there aren't any...

2. **Dilemma:** a situation with no good options. This gives your reader a chance to worry, which is good. Your reader must be wondering what can possibly happen next. Let your POV character work through the choices. Let him sort things out.

3. **Decision:** the act of making a choice among several options. This is important, because it lets your POV character become proactive again. People who never make decisions aren't interesting. So make your character decide, and make it a good decision. Make it one your reader can respect. Make it risky, but make it have a chance of working. Do that, and your reader will have to turn the page, because now your POV character has a new Goal.

And now you've come full circle. You've gone from **Scene** to **Sequel** and back to the Goal for a new **Scene**.

Plot Structure—Thematic Story Arc

Wendy Webb, in *The Gila Queen's Guide to Markets*, talks about a "Seven-Point" plot structure, based on theme and protagonist story arc, which goes like this:

- Hook
- Problem
- Backfill
- Complication
- Action
- The Dark Moment
- Resolution

This step-wise plot approach reflects the three-act elements of the "Hero's Journey", discussed in Chapter J.

Plot & Story—The KISS Principle

Plot drives the story. It is "the engine drawing everything else along," says Dibell. "If you weigh it down with too much exposition, it's going to grind to a wheezing halt." What Dibell is saying is that you need to balance thematic elements that involve character intro-spection, setting description and illumination with the movement of storytelling, which is plot.

Readers, Dibell says, are only interested in explanation *after* their curiosity has already been aroused by something that needs explaining.

Introduce your character, let her act and show herself, engage a reader's sympathies and curiosity, says Dibell. *Then* tell her background, if you need to. It comes down to "show and tell" (see Chapter T).

Plotting the Journey

Dibell reminds us that "plot is a verb". Plot moves. It takes you somewhere; it takes you on a journey. Something is happening or going to happen. The main plot, which runs through the entire story is usually what the story opens with and provides the final climax or confrontation near the end. It's what you promise in the beginning when you open with your main character doing or experiencing something. Dibell gives the example of Ralph finding the conch shell on the beach in *Lord of the Flies*. Piggy instructs Ralph to blow the shell, bringing all the other castaways together. The shell becomes the symbol of leadership and the power struggle, characterizing each boy. The conch is introduced, along with the main character, in the beginning and is destroyed in the climax near the end.

Bill Johnson said that every story makes a promise at the beginning to the reader. Those promises, says Dibell, are mostly unspoken ones. And some are made indirectly through pattern. As the journey continues, problems build on the previous ones, always moving the main plot toward the final crisis. "The job of a middle," says Dibell, "is to build toward and deliver crisis."

"Detail on detail, incident on incident, character

151

on character, the pattern(s) begin to form," says Dibell "...they're what hold your story together, give it both diversity and unity."

Dibell describes plot as a tapestry of pattern, form, shape and color that share recognizable meanings. Which brings me to subplots, the threads that make up the story's fabric.

Subplots, Parallel Plotlines & Patterns

Subplots are more common in long fiction, where they are used to deepen a story and add layers that make it more intriguing and tease out more depth to the story. Subplots may provide varying aspects of a theme, from community to individual as played out by different characters. Ultimately, subplots and how they are crafted, provide the writer with the means to transcend plot into what Dibell calls *pattern*.

Dibell describes "braided" plots, in which two or more subplots are woven together, and parallel plotlines, in which two plots share almost equal footing. This happens when strong protagonists carry each plot. Parallel plotlines often run counterpoint to each other in pace, tone and color. Each plot becomes richer and stronger when contrasted with the other. And they are always connected in some way, in many ways.

In *Matrix Reloaded*, Neo's introspective and thoughtful plot with the architect of the matrix runs counterpoint with Trinity's action plot as she sabotages the matrix and battles an agent. Both demonstrate conflict and tension but the tone and pace are opposite. This contrast only heightens each plot line. Notice also how the two plot lines are connected and eventually converge in the final scene where Neo saves Trinity's life by restarting her heart. Earlier on, while Trinity is totally engrossed in her problems, Neo becomes aware of her struggle through the architect's artful hint; this prompts Neo to choose his path to join her plot. His awareness is the bridge between the two plotlines. If you look carefully, you will find many other ways the two plotlines are connected, visually, mentally and viscerally and how they inevitably draw together in that riveting last scene; "how thoroughly," Dibell says, "the story belongs to itself."

"If you stop thinking in terms of *things* and start thinking in *categories of things*," says Dibell, "you'll see more resemblances, echoes, and outright repetitions in your favorite fiction than you'd ever suspected."

Mirrored Pattern on the Wall...

Scenes, characters, and plots can be mirrored. This process starts with identifying two situations that can be tagged for connection and built-in recurrence. Mirrored plots often run as double stories concurrently or through alternating flashback narration. Good examples include *The Empire Strikes Back, Wuthering Heights* and *Lord of the Rings*. My short story, *The Arc of Time* used a double plot set 40,000 years apart, one played out with real characters and the other in the form of e-letters between two lovers. Both plots converged in the end.

Mirrored plots are achieved by setting up pairs of

opposite and/or complimentary scenes that share emotional resonance.

Dibell provides these hints to create effective mirroring scenes:

- Repeat one or more lines of dialogue (e.g. the "I love you," "I know," between Han and Leia in *Star Wars*)
- Repeat a brief description of emotion
- Have the two situations go through similar stages
- Use similar imagery
- Ensure that subject and terms are the same
- Keep the polarities/emotional content the same

Ultimately, the pattern that develops forms a moving story that has rhythm and cadence.

Ten Commandments for Plotting

Crawford Kilian, SF writer and author of *Writing Science Fiction and Fantasy*, set down these ten commandments:

- Nothing should happen at random
- Plot stems from character under adversity
- Give each character an urgent personal agenda
- The plot of a story is the synthesis of the plots of its individual characters
- The plot "begins" long before the story
- Foreshadow all important elements

- Keep in mind the kind of story you're telling
- Ironic plots subvert their surface meanings
- The hero must eventually take charge of events
- Plot dramatizes character.

References

Bell, James Scott. 2004. *Plot & Structure: (Techniques And Exercises For Crafting A Plot That Grips Readers From Start To Finish)*. Writer's Digest Books. Cincinnati, Ohio. 240pp.

Bickham, Jack. 1993. *Elements of Fiction Writing: Scene and Structure*. Writer's Digest Books. Cincinnati, Ohio.

Boles, Paul Darcy. 1987. *Storycrafting*. North Light Books.

Dibell, Ansen. 1999. *Elements of Fiction Writing: Plot*. Writer's Digest Books. Cincinnati, Ohio. 170pp.

Hodgins, Jack. 2001. *A Passion for Narrative*. McClelland and Stewart. 320pp.

Ingermanson, Randy. 2008. "Writing the Perfect Scene". In: *Advanced Fiction Writing.com*. http://www.advancedfictionwriting.com/art/scene

Kilian, Crawford. 2003. "Ten Points on Plotting". In: *Writing Fiction*: http://crofsblogs.typepad.com/fiction/2003/07/ten_points_on_p.html

Swain, Dwight. 1982. *Techniques of the Selling Writer*. University of Oklahoma Press. 330pp.

Q. ● Queries & Other Quests

The query for the novel is the single most important piece of paper a novelist writes
—James Axtell

"On the surface, query letters look simple," Elizabeth Lyon, author of *The Sell Your Novel Toolkit*, remarks. "After all, they are only letters of enquiry; Writer seeks agent or editor interested in novel. A query's sole purpose is to gain a request to see the manuscript. So simple...Not so simple."

A query letter is your letter of enquiry to a publisher/editor or agent regarding the possible publication or representation of your work. "It's a writer's introduction, our calling card and, hopefully, our foot in the door," says Lynn Flewelling, author of *Luck in the Shadows*. "Some agents and editors glance at the letter but read the chapters first," she adds. "Others read the query and reject the chapters unseen if the letter doesn't sing. You never know, so write the letter like it's the one thing standing between you and success. It just might be."

While query letters are very important for novelists, they are not always necessary if you are writing short stories or magazine articles (unless the publisher specifies the need for one in their submission guidelines); just submit your short story with a brief introductory cover letter. This is less hassle for you and works faster in the long run.

Where a query is required, it is important to write a good one. This is often the very first and only item an editor will see to make a decision to look at more of your writing.

Literary agents and editors get thousands of query letters a year and any writer would readily admit that queries are an art form unto themselves. Agents and editors are also the first to acknowledge the capriciousness and subjectivity of their selection  process. "You can't control rejections based on the personal tastes of agents and editors," says Lyon. "However, you can learn to craft queries that are well-written and clear enough to attract the interest of an agent or editor who does like your ideas."

Parts of a Query Letter

In her book, *The Sell Your Novel Toolkit*, Lyon dissects the query into:

- **Lead:** using a **creative hook** (direct immersion in the story; discussion of the period, setting or milieu; or presentation of the theme of the book) or business hook (with particulars about the book, comparisons with others, and author's credentials and awards)

- **Body:** short synopsis, either story- or characterization/theme-focused; brief biography with credentials, etc.

- **Conclusion:** closing sentences; the "handshake"

Lyon also covers style, types and uses, with examples, including unconventional queries, email queries and query packages (e.g., pros and cons of featuring a one-page standard query accompanied by one-to-two page synopsis, separate author biography, and testimonials). Lyon then devotes a whole chapter to examples of successful queries, with running commentary on why they are.

Many successful writers who submit online queries use a less formal approach, typical of email format. John Hewitt of *Poe War, Writer's Resource Centre*, considers the formal query an advantage whether submitted online or in the mail; he suggests that "a well-written query letter helps prove to an editor that you are qualified to write the piece."

Research Your Target

Assuming that you've already done your overall marketing and have established that the target is applicable to your writing subject, you need to further research the specific publication. Study the publication's masthead for a current editor's name. Don't just rely on *Writer's Market*, or other similar publications; they will likely be out of date. Editors move around. Always get the writer's guidelines for the specific publication. If  these are not readily available, ask for them. Depending on whether it is an agent, magazine or book editor you're targeting, they may wish to see anything from just a query to a synopsis and partial submission as well. Many have specifications on format too. Addressing these will put you ahead of many people who don't bother to do this initial legwork.

Polish & Be Professional

- Ensure that there are no spelling or grammatical errors
- Make sure your editor's name is correct as well as the publication name and address
- Use standard letter format and standard paper (keep it simple and professional) and stay away from fancy patterns or colored paper
- Keep the letter to one page if possible
- Include a self-addressed stamped envelope (SASE) for mailed queries
- Include your name, postal address, email address and phone number

Hook their Interest

"When an author sends in a query for a novel, the hook is the crucial element," writes Chuck Sambuchino, editor of "Guide to Literary Agents", in *Writer's Digest* (October, 2008). "[The] agent [or editor] wants to know what makes the particular book unique."

Your query should introduce a fresh idea or topic and be presented at the beginning of your letter. The idea is to excite the editor.

Show Confidence & Be Persuasive

Be succinct and direct. Make your statements simply and without hype.

- Provide any credentials or awards (including nominations) you have received, particularly those relevant to the subject you are writing about. If you've received many, pick the best ones
- Include a list of publications you've published
- Close your letter with a polite statement like: "I look forward to hearing from you."

You may include a short writing sample relevant to the publication to provide a good example of your writing.

What DOESN'T Work...

John Hewitt provides a good list of what NOT to

do in a query letter. Here are a few:

- Don't mention who has rejected the piece before
- Don't apologize for any weaknesses
- Don't ask for advice, comments or criticism/analysis
- Don't gush about how excited you are about being published
- Don't go on about this being your first
- Don't include a lot of personal information about yourself
- Don't provide several projects in the same query, unless they are related and part of a series
- Don't query the same editor twice
- Don't discuss copyright information, or payment
- Don't include inappropriate off-subject samples

Mark Juddery (in *Writer's Digest*'s, "Writer's Yearbook Extra", 2001) wrote a marvelous article on the most famous query letter in history—the lyrics of *Paperback Writer* by the Beatles—to demonstrate by negative example some of the common pitfalls a beginning writer may slide into. Given my love for this particular song (despite its lyrics, it inspired me ever since I was a little girl) I thought I would use it to do the same:

Dear Sir or Madam, will you read my book? This cavalier approach suggests a lack of effort on your part and puts you on the wrong foot right away.

161

There's no excuse for not knowing the name of your relevant contact. This is easily researched these days through Internet, market digests (available at libraries) or by browsing actual books.

It took me years to write, will you take a look?

This kind of hyperbole does not impress editors. They are well aware how much work it takes to produce a piece of polished writing; you are better off with a professional approach that is less pleading and more matter-of-fact.

...based on a novel by a man named Lear

While it may work well to draw parallels with other works or people, this strikes as being unoriginal, possibly plagiarized and will be less attractive to the editor. Watch what details you choose to share; less is more sometimes.

And I need a job, so I want to be a paperback writer...

More of that pleading tone and hyperbole; the editor knows this already.

It's the dirty story of a dirty man, and his clinging wife doesn't understand.

All queries need to tell the editor what the book is about; however, this should be original, and entice the editor to read more in as few words as possible. This is the most important part of the query and should be the part where you spend most of your time.

His son is working for the Daily Mail.

The second sentence should build on the first with detail and further enlightenment and something juicy. If it's not diverting, don't include it; again, less is more.

I can make it longer if you like the style, I can change it round...

First off, this shows a lack of confidence; you've just sent the work in and are already offering to change it! While it is good to demonstrate the willingness to work with editors and revise, this is also a given if you are a professional. So, again, you shouldn't have to state this; rather, show it indirectly with your past history, credentials and work you've done.

It could make a million for you overnight

This kind of statement sends editors running. It is not the writer's place to suggest how successful the book will be; however, you may suggest reasons for its **potential** success, by citing current and relevant trends.

The bottom line is: be professional. Get to the point and use words sparingly. Whatever you say in the query needs to have purpose. "Cute" sometimes works but you better know your editor and you better know him or her by name!

What DOES Work...

So, that was a letter that didn't work. Below is an example of one that did work. It's a query letter that Robert J. Sawyer, Hugo and Nebula-winning science fiction author, wrote to land his agent. He provides this skeletized version on his website, which also has many other resources for beginning writers.

Dear *[Agent's Name]:*
I hope you will be interested in taking me on as a new client. I have completed a science fiction novel called [title] which I would like you to represent.

[Two sentences of description of the novel, avoiding hype]
As a sample of my work, I've enclosed a copy of the September 1988 issue of *Amazing Stories*, which has my novelette "Golden Fleece" as the cover story. "Golden Fleece" has made it to the preliminary Nebula Award ballot. *[If you've got something impressive you can show him/her up front, do so — but don't send the novel manuscript until asked to do so.]*

[Two more short paragraphs summarizing your other credentials, if relevant; I mentioned my successful non-fiction writing career...]

I intend to produce a lot of books. I'm already hard at work on my second. *[Agents have no use for one-book clients, since almost all first novels sell for peanuts — the agent makes no real money unless you have an on-going career.]* I'm approaching you before I query any other agents because I've been impressed by your columns in *Locus*. Having an agent who so clearly understands the forces that are shaping publishing is something I consider crucial. *[Let the agent know why you're approaching him/her — something more than "I saw your name in* Writer's Digest.*"]*

I would very much like to send you [title] for your consideration. SASE enclosed.

In her article, *The Complete Nobody's Guide to Query Letters*, Lynn Flewelling gives another good example of a successful query letter. Here are some of the points she makes in hers:

- **Opening:** Make sure you're writing to the right person and you spell their name right (addressing your query to someone who left the agency three years ago doesn't look good).
- **First Paragraph:** a brief statement of what you're selling, how long it is and that it's complete (which it should be, particularly for a first novel). Here's an example from Lynn Flewelling: "I am seeking representation for my fantasy adventure novel, *Luck In The Shadows*, complete at 170,000 words." She goes on to add that she's included a synopsis and opening chapters (mentioned in the agency's submission guidelines) and has a sequel and other book in the works, which shows that she is a serious writer

with ambition for a career.

- **Second Paragraph:** Lynn's "why I wrote the book"
- **Third Paragraph**: a brief synopsis of the book, which introduces the main protagonist, theme and premise and anything that makes the book stand out as unique. This is also your chance to demonstrate your writing skill.
- **Fourth Paragraph:** your experience and background. Say's Lynn: "Got it? Flaunt it! Don't got it? Keep quiet." Her point is to make any background relevant and credible.
- **Last Paragraph:** the standard good-bye that should be polite, short and professsional.

References

Flewelling, Lynn. 2005. The Complete Nobody's Guide to Query Letters. In: Science Fiction Writers of America. http://www.sfwa.org/writing/query

Hewit, John. "How to Write a Query Letter." In: *Poe War, Writer's Resource Centre*. http://www.poewar.com/how-to-write-a-query

Juddery, Mark. 2001. "How *Not* to be a Paperback Writer". In: *Writer's Yearbook Extra*, Writer's Digest. 2001.

Sambuchino, Chuck. 2008. "A Successful Aftermath". *Writer's Digest*, October, 2008.

Sawyer, Robert J. SF Writer: http://www.sfwriter.com/index.htm

R. ♥ How to Reject Rejection Letters

If at first you don't succeed, try, try again. Then Quit. There's no need being a fool about it
—W.C. Fields

We've all suffered rejection and disappointment. Perhaps that job you coveted or someone you loved who might have even led you on before dropping you. It hurts. But you move on. And it does get better. It does, trust me.

In a 1999 article in *Writer's Journal*, Dennis E. Hensley, associate professor of English at Taylor University Fort Wayne and author of *Writing for Profit*, told the story of  when his writing teacher in college tried to console him after a short story of his had been rejected for the umpteenth time. "Listen," she had said, "**you** weren't rejected, your **manuscript** was." He didn't quite see it that way. "It was **my** title, **my** lead, **my** characters, **my** plot and **my** ending," he'd responded. "No one else had anything to do with it. If the story was rejected, then let's face it: as a writer, I was rejected." Rejection is still rejection. Thirty years later, Hensley adds that he still gets rejection letters and he is still not overjoyed to receive them.

As time goes on and you become a more seasoned writer, you develop a business-attitude and an objective way of viewing rejection letters. The irony is that it is the beginner writer who is more likely to get rejections.

Surviving Rejection

Children's writer Margot Finke challenges you with these questions:

- Can you allow someone else to bring in the mail every day?
- Can you still smile after receiving three rejection letters in a row?
- Are you regularly sending out completed manuscripts?
- Can you fight off the tears when your husband (or wife) says 'But Sweetie, it doesn't matter, I still love you!' "???

If your answer is yes, then you have graduated from the "I Will Become a Published Author" school of rejection with honors, she says. If not, keep reading!

Rejection is Step One of a Journey to Publication

Think of rejection as part of a road to success. The bottom line is that if you have never been rejected then you haven't really tried, have you?

Rejection really is the first step toward acceptance. With anything that is worth doing, there is risk and there is vulnerability. So too in writing (see Chapter Z). In order to publish, you have to risk being rejected. In fact, count on it. YOUR WORK WILL BE REJECTED. The good news is that at some point your work will also BE ACCEPTED; count on that too.

But I'm getting ahead of myself again. In order to take that first step on the road to being a published writer, you need to accept that it will be a bumpy road with dips (rejections) and puddles (nasty rejections) but also wonderful paved sections (publishing contracts!). When you decide to take that road to publish your work you accept all parts of that road, not just the paved sections. In fact, usually the road starts out as a dirt road (like a lot of things in life). The important part is to have a healthy view of your commitment. This means looking at rejection letters as your introduction to the publishing world.

Hensley shares several excellent insights on how to gain a good perspective and view rejecttions to your advantage.

View #1: view selling manuscripts as a "cold call" business and therefore treat it that way too (see below under *Make Rejection Work for You*). Selling manuscripts, like a door-to-door salesman, often means approaching editors you've never met. I've sold many of my manuscripts, even books, to people I never met (I still haven't met the editor of my first book, whose office is in Indianapolis—I live in Canada). Until you establish a relationship with your market (and you will), selling becomes a numbers game. The more you send the more likely you are to get a hit. It's all in the statistics. You need to treat it that way. See my example of short story submissions below.

View #2: view rejections as an opportunity. Rejections can provide the opportunity to learn and re-evaluate, usually of appropriate market and publisher subjectivity rather than writing quality. I know this to be true based on my experience of short story submission (see below under *Make Rejection Work for You*). Essentially, after two publishers had seen both stories A and B, one publisher preferred story A and called story B boring, while the other publisher found story B riveting and disliked story A. Go figure! It's all in personal preference and markets. Hensley talks about having written a short story about two professional hunters stalking one another. After many detective and mystery magazines rejected it, someone suggested he send it to a literary quarterly (because the story was about characters, their emotions and desire to succeed). It was accepted right away. I'm getting ahead of myself again, because now we're talking about marketing and that's a whole other guidebook.

View #3: view rejections as the beginning of a relationship. Not all rejections are final; in fact most aren't. Most times a rejection stems from story redundancy, lack of space or editorial requirements. They really ARE only rejecting the piece, not YOU. Remember, publishers wouldn't be in the business if it weren't for writers. They'd be idiots to reject YOU. Read your letter very carefully. If it is a personalized letter rather than a form letter (which is a very good sign, by the way!) take what they say as gospel. If the editor says "the ending needs work" that's what they mean and often they are also open to re-submission after revision. When I submitted my story *A Butterfly in Peking* to Chiaroscuro, they actually rejected it but added a caveat and an invite to resubmit. I did and they accepted the revised story, which went on to earn accolades and was translated and reprinted into several languages. Similarly, an editor may say something like: "Thanks, but this wasn't a match for us...Do try us again." They mean it. It means they liked your writing but the story wasn't right (they may have run something too similar to it already or it didn't fit with the other pieces or theme or whatever, etc.) and they want to see more of your work. It's an invitation to submit. Take it! You've made contact.

View #4: view rejections as part of your success journey. You are in good company (see below under *Cheer Up...You're in Good Company*). Rejection is a given in the writing business where often a story may be considered "before its time", untried, a risk and therefore harder to place. This is often why a book that was rejected so many times becomes a great hit once it does get published—the very quality that made it hard for a traditional publisher to accept made it a success with the readership: because it was extremely original, new and refreshing. In my area of writing, slipstream or what's called "cross-genre" pieces are often passed over because they are considered too risky to market (see Chapter G). Yet, when one does get published it provides something fresh to a readership eager for something new. What does this mean? It means KEEP TRYING! DON'T GIVE UP!

View #5: view rejections as your first step to success. It means that you've graduated from "talking writer" to "writing writer". When I tell people that I write books, many of them will eagerly respond with their own great book idea or intention to write some day when they've re-tired and finished their "real" job. The reality is that thinking about writing and actually writing are two very different things. Writing is hard work and publishing is more of the same. The romanticized view of writing that memoir or best seller quickly vanishes once a would-be writer sits down and begins the task. So, getting that first rejection in the mail is a great affirmation that you have taken that first significant step to becoming a serious writer. Congratulations! Be proud and know that you will succeed.

Don't Miss the Good Stuff!

Okay...so you received another rejection letter. Once you've let yourself react emotionally and had that cup of coffee or tea, reread that letter. Read every word carefully, especially if it is a personalized latter, rather than a form letter. Chances are, the rejection isn't a full-blown rejection. Chances are, they've invited you to submit again. Or at least they've left it open for you to submit again. Most rejection letters include such a line, even some form letters. These people are in the business of publishing, after all, and you are a potential contributor. Without you they wouldn't have a business.

Rejection letters are LETTERS; letters of introduction, in fact. Letters represent a communication between you and your potential publisher. A rejection letter often represents the first communication of an ongoing relationship between you and your publisher. Yes, I said "you and your publisher"; because often an **acceptance begins with a rejection**.

Because of this, it's important to read every word as objectively as you can. And treat it as the first step of a successful business venture.

Here are some examples of rejection letter notes I've received and what they mean:

What They Said:	Which Means:
"not a good match for us"	Something about your story didn't match up with the theme, layout or topics handled by the publication—you need to research this before submitting something else to them. Read the publication!
"This tale didn't quite work for me, I'm afraid"	They either published something like it or it just isn't to their taste. Do more research before submitting something else to them. Submit elsewhere.
"The plot didn't quite hold me"	The story was too long and/or had too much exposition and/or not enough action for that pub-

	lication. Research the market and resubmit elsewhere. If you get this twice look carefully at your plot elements.
"**I'm afraid this story didn't quite come alive for me...**"	See above comments.
"**...your work does not suit our needs at present.**"	They likely published something similar already or your work doesn't match their current theme. Research the publication before submitting more to them.

You get the picture. Most of the comments point to market decisions; not to your writing. For *Arc of Time*, I'd received several rejections, with notes like those above, before three paying markets, including a magazine in Greece, accepted the story (which I had not revised!).

The Evolution of "Rejection"

I have personally experienced an evolution in rejection letters, whether because of my improving writing, or improving marketing or both. Here's how they evolved:

Lowest form: the form letter, with no name or signature—you get nothing from this except that they're too busy to even go to the bathroom probably! Don't sweat it. File the letter and try them again with another story; you can even play a game of it to see how many submissions it takes to get "recognized". Meantime send the rejected story elsewhere.

Next lowest form: Personalized form letter with

your name on it and a name and signature on it. Congratulations! You are now a person. And you will likely be remembered when you submit another story here.

Higher on the Evolutionary Path: a form letter that includes a personalized note about your work and why it was rejected (often with an added comment about the story or your writing). WOW! You have made a mark. Try them again!

Even Higher on the Evolutionary Path: a personalized letter that explains why your story was rejected—this says as much about the editor as it does about how they felt about your story; they are taking the time to give you feedback means you are worth it to them. You have an opportunity to begin a relationship with this editor. Play fair.

Highest on the Path: a personalized, perhaps even handwritten, note that specifies why they rejected your piece with suggestions for revision (and resubmission) or invitation to submit another piece. Congratulations! This is the beginning of a relationship. Revise and resubmit. You're there!

What Rejection Letters Look Like

As I've already mentioned, I've received a lot of rejection letters in the many years of my writing career. They've ranged from the short card form letter with no signature to the handwritten, personalized letter with inviting comments.

Zoetrope
ALL STORY

Thank you very much
for submitting your
manuscript to *Zoetrope:
All-Story.*

We appreciate your
interest and regret
that we are unable to
use your story.

The Editors

Rejection letters will vary as much as the magazine and book market varies. The larger, busier companies that receive many more submissions over a given time period are more likely to go with the form letter. I've heard some agents and editors go this route simply because it is safer for them. One magazine editor lamented to me not long ago that after she had provided a writer whose work she'd rejected with several paragraphs of explanation, the said writer had responded with an irascible diatribe of her skills as an editor.

Take heart: receiving a form letter like the one above from Zoetrope is very common, particularly from a large publisher. And take it for what it is, a letter that gives you very little information other than they rejected your story. File the letter and send the story elsewhere.

Some publishers and agents use a checklist, which can provide you with very good feedback (see example below from Challenging Destiny for my short story, *Arc of Time* which found a home in several places after this rejection).

Challenging Destiny
47 Bridgeport Rd E
Waterloo, ON
Canada N2J 2J4

csp@golden.net
http://home.golden.net/~csp/

Aug 3/02

Greetings,

I have decided not to use your story in *Challenging Destiny*. I read all the stories that are submitted myself, and I unfortunately don't have time to read to the end of each story. To give you some idea of how interesting I found your story, here's how much of it I read.

☐ One page.
☐ A few pages.
☐ Most of the story.
☑ The entire story.

I've checked off below my reason(s) for not using your story.

☐ There were too many spelling and grammar mistakes.

☐ The story is a short-short story, and I just don't use very many of them.
☐ I don't use horror stories.
☐ The science fiction or fantasy aspect isn't very strong in the story.

☐ I didn't care enough about the characters.

☐ The opening of the story didn't grab me.
☐ You've got a lot of telling in the story and not enough showing.
☐ I found the story confusing.
☐ I found the ending anticlimactic.
☐ There wasn't enough "meat" in the story to merit its length.
☐ The story didn't have anything new to offer.
☐ I didn't buy the premise of the story.
☑ You've got some interesting ideas here, but the story didn't quite "do it" for me.

☐ There wasn't anything wrong with the story—it just didn't rise above some of the others I've received recently.

Thanks for letting me look at your work, and good luck in the future.

Sincerely,

Dave

Dave Switzer
Editor

The letter on the next page that rejected my short story *Angel of Chaos* (which later turned into *Butterfly in Peking*) provided enough insight to why they didn't choose it that I could have gone one of two ways: 1) I could have left the story as it was and submitted elsewhere; or 2) I could have emailed them with a suggestion that

I'd be willing to revise if they would reconsider a revision according to their specifications. I've done this in the past and published. This time I decided not to because I liked the story the way it was.

Space & Time
138 West 70th Street (4B)
New York, NY 10023-4468
http://www.cith.org/space&time.html

June 20, 2002

Dear Ms. Munteanu:

Thanks for sending "Angel Of Chaos" to Space & Time. I regret to say we won't be using it. While it was well written, I felt that the expalnation you tacked on at the end should have been developed as part of the story.

Best of luck placing it elsewhere, and thanks again for considering Space & Time.

Best Wishes,

Amy Benesch

Amy Benesch, Associate Editor

One magazine I submitted to gives your story to two independent readers whose comments they include along with their rejection or acceptance. This is great feedback for you! What I found frustratingly amusing was that the accolades of the reviewers didn't guarantee the acceptance of my story. While my story *Arc of Time* generated very positive comments from both reviewers, the magazine still decided against publishing and the rejection letter gave no reason (see reviewer's comments below):

Reviewer #1: "*I love the way this story is set up, switching back and forth from the different points of view. The "trippiness" is very appealing and* *works well with the modern/fantastical contrast."*

Reviewer #2: *"This was an intriguing and extraordinary clever story. I didn't have a clue about the jape at the end until I got to the last page. And then it unfolded beautifully. The theological tie-ins were smart and fun and showed either some Mormon extrapolative thought or extreme knowledge of Biblical lore."*

You'd have thought, eh? But they rejected anyway. Below is an example of a form letter with a handwritten comment added along with signature and an invite to try them again.

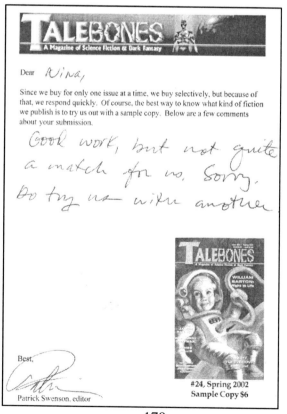

Make Rejection Work For You

One way to see your way through rejection is to find ways to distance yourself from your story once you've sent it off and to see the whole process of submission-rejection-acceptance as a business. The very best way to do this is to submit lots of stories and to keep submitting them. With novels, this is a little harder to do but you can certainly be working on the next one once you've submitted the first.

When I was writing short stories, I kept a list of  what and where I submitted, along with the most important item: where to submit NEXT. At any given time, I made sure that I had at least x-number of submissions out there and each story had a designated place to go if it returned. As soon as a story came back from magazine A, I simply re-packaged it and sent it to magazine B. The critical part of the list was to have a contingency for each story: the next place where I would send the story once it returned. I was planning on the story being rejected with the hope that it would be accepted; that way, a rejection became part of a story's journey rather than a final comment.

I ran my submissions like a bus terminal. A story was in and out so fast it never had a chance to cool off. And, since I had five other pieces out there, I could do this with little emotion. I was running a fast-paced "story depot", after all. All my stories had to be out there as soon as possible; if they were sitting in the terminal, they were doing nothing for me.

Cheer up...You're in Good Company...

Take heart in the fact that virtually every writer has had something of theirs rejected, in some cases many times, before getting it accepted. For instance, *Jonathan Livingston Seagull* was rejected twenty-three times; *Dune* twenty-one times; and *The Hunt for Red October* eighteen times before being accepted by a publisher.

Irving Stone's *Lust for Life* was rejected sixteen times before a publisher finally picked it up and sold about twenty-five million copies. Not bad for a story that was passed off as: "A long, dull novel about an artist."

Beatrix Potter's *The Tale of Peter Rabbit* was turned down so many times that she initially self-published.

J.K. Rowling's first Harry Potter book had been rejected by eight publishers before Bloomsbury bought it for a £2,500 advance.

Andre Bernard published a collection of rejection letters sent by publishers to now famous authors of classic books. *Rotten Rejections: The Letters that Publishers Wish They'd Never Sent*, includes rejection letters to Henry James, Gertrude Stein and Joseph Heller. Books publishers have overlooked prior to finally getting accepted include: *War and Peace*, *The Good*

Earth, *To Kill a Mockingbird*, *Watership Down*, among many others.

Rejection is, in fact, part of success. Every rejection is a step closer to publication.

Here are Some Great Rejections!

Check out these great examples of rejections received by now-famous authors and their books:

- Dr. Seuss: "Too different from other juveniles on the market to warrant its selling."

- *Lady Chatterley's Lover* by D.H. Lawrence: "For your own sake do not publish this book."

- *The Wind in the Willows* by Kenneth Grahame: "An irresponsible holiday story."

- *Lord of the Flies* by William Golding: "An absurd and uninteresting fantasy which was rubbish and dull."

- *The Diary of Anne Frank*: "the girl doesn't, it seems to me, have a special perception or feeling which would lift that book above the curiosity level."

- *The Spy who Came in from the Cold* by John le Carré: "You're welcome to le Carré—he hasn't got any future."

- *Lolita* by Vladimir Nabokov: "...over-whelmingly nauseating, even to an enlightened Freudian...the whole thing is an unsure cross between hideous reality and improbably fantasy. It often becomes a wild neurotic daydream...I recommend that it be buried under a stone for a thousand years."

Something Worse Than Rejection

Now, what could that possibly be? I see your brow wrinkling in thought. The answer is: acceptance by the wrong publication. Let me give you one example in my legacy of foolish mistakes in submission (corner me in the bar of a writing convention and I'll tell you more).

Several years ago, when I was first submitting short stories everywhere, I was using several online market listings to find possible fits to my science fiction stories. I ended up submitting *Angel's Promises* to Magazine A, among others (as part of a simultaneous submission, which is okay so long as you let them know) and I received a letter that the story was accepted and would appear in a particular issue. While I was waiting for Magazine A to publish my piece I got an acceptance from another publisher. I told them that it was appearing in Magazine A but they were welcome to second printing rights when they became available and the timing was right. Luckily, Magazine B was amenable. Why was I lucky, you ask? Because Magazine A never did publish my piece and when I finally got a look at their magazine, it turned out to be a stapled photocopy of newspaper clippings with a few hand-typed pieces. Luckily Magazine B was *Dreams & Visions* and my story went on to garner a nomination for the Speculative Literature Foundation's Fountain award and then was selected to appear in that publisher's "Best of" Anthology.

Lesson Learned: KNOW YOUR MARKET! (And read *The Alien's Cool Guide to Fiction Markets* by Pixl Press).

References

Bernard, Andre. 2002. *Rotten Rejections: The Letters that Publishers Wish They'd Never Sent.* Robson Books Ltd. 102pp.

Finke, Margot. 2008. "How to Keep Your Passion and Survive as a Writer." In: *The Purple Crayon*, http://www.underdown.org/mf_writing_passion.htm

Hensley, Dennis E. 1999. "Five New Ways of Viewing Rejection Letters". In: *Writer's Journal*, November/December, 1999.

S. ❤ Get Sensual...And What About SEX?

We have five major senses and several minor ones we aren't even consciously aware of. The major ones are sight, hearing, smell, touch, and taste.

In the April 2000 issue of *Fiction Writer* Janet Fitch, author of *White Oleander*, tells us that we are biologically and psychologically designed "for intense experience in a richly sensual world. But we find ourselves in a senses-depleted world, a world limited largely to visuals, and *ersatz* ones at that." She suggests that our readers are starving for sensual information. "For fiction writers, the senses are not only a window onto external reality, but also the gateway into the inner realms."

As writers we are in a unique position (at least for now) to describe what the visual media can't (yet). We can provide our readers with a rich spectrum of sensuality such as what a place smells like, the texture of an object, the taste of a food, as well as the nuances of light and sound. Readers don't just "watch" a character in a book; they enter the character's body and "feel".

So, how do writers satisfy the readers' need to experience the senses fully? Description, yes. But how cold is cold? What does snow really

185

smell like? What color is that sunset? How do you describe the taste of wine to a teetotaler?

Ultimately, literal description doesn't quite cut it. To have the sense really sink in and linger with the reader, it should be linked to the emotions and memories of the character experiencing it. By doing this, you are achieving several things at the same time:

- You're describing the sense as the character is experiencing it—emotionally
- You're revealing additional information on the character through his/her reaction
- You're likely creating a more compelling link for the reader's own experience of the sense

How is this done? There are several tools a writer may use to achieve this. Here are a few:

- Use metaphor (see also Chapter M) to describe the sense
- Link the sense to memories
- Use synesthesia (cross-sensory metaphor) to describe the sense
- Link the sense psychologically to an emotion or attitude
- Relate to the sense in a different way (e.g., a visual scene from the point of view of a painter)

Metaphor

The most compelling fiction arises when "truth" is portrayed obliquely, when objects or scenes are described through "impression", or what I call truth-interpreted, rather than through literal description. Janet Fitch recommends that you "come in at an angle, the way you approach all things evanescent." This is where metaphor plays an important role. Of course, it goes without saying that for this to work, the writer must use appropriate metaphors. I talk more about this in the section on SEX scenes, below.

The use of metaphor when used to describe an object or place through one or several senses adds a dimension of emotion, tone and direction.

The richest, most vivid words, says Fitch, are those that use more than one sense at a time. She compares the term "yellow sky", which provides one sense (vision) to a "lemon sky", which gives you not only a visual sense but suggests taste, smell and even texture. The metaphor of "lemon" suggests an emotional as well as a vivid sensual description.

Smell and Memory

While all five of our senses can be linked to memories, two of them stand out. Smell and taste let us sample the chemicals around us for information. According to the California Institute of Technology, smell is generally considered the sense tied most closely to human memory, profoundly influencing people's ability to recall past events and experiences. "Memory lies coiled within us like a magician's trick handkerchief, and a simple smell or taste can pluck the tiniest corner and pull out the world," says Fitch.

"Smell is different from all the other senses in a very special way. A smell from your distant past can unleash a flood of memories that are so intense and striking that they seem real," says Dr. Karl (Kruszelnicki), author of *Great Moments in Science* (1984) and science host of *ABC Radio* (Australia). "This kind of memory, where an unexpected re-encounter with a scent from the distant past brings back a rush of memories, is called a 'Proustian Memory'", based on Marcel Proust's sensual description of the smell of a madeleine cake dipped into lime-blossom tea in *Swan's Way*, the first volume of his novel, *Remembrance of Things Past*.

The sense of smell was no doubt one of the first senses to evolve in living creatures; it told us what was safe to eat. It also affects behavior, such as finding a mate, synchronizing menstrual cycles, and communicating with the other animals in your group. Dr. Karl tells us that "women can tell (by the smell of swabs taken from the armpit) who has been watching happy or sad movies (men are not so good at this). A breast-feeding baby can differentiate the smell of his or her mother, from any other nursing mother. Dogs and horses can smell fear in humans."

Ironically, smell, along with taste, is often neglected in our own overt observations and in writing. By consciously attending to these two senses alone, the writer is assured of engaging the reader's more deeply rooted sensuality.

It might be useful to list some of your best remembered favorite or most powerful smells. Here are some that my family members and I came up with over the dinner table:

- Freshly cut grass
- My lover's neck
- Cold snow
- The interior of a new car
- Baking bread
- Wood burning fireplace
- Forest just after a rainstorm
- Freshly shampooed hair
- My own pillow
- My cat when he just comes in from outside

Exercise:

7. Think of a childhood memory that inspires powerful emotions. Describe it from as many senses as you can remember.

8. List at least ten of your favorite smells. Use at least two of them in the context of a story you are working on.

9. Take one of them and describe it from the POV of several people with different emotional states and/or cultural backgrounds.

Synesthesia

Synesthesia uses one sense to describe another. It is a powerful tool in the hands of a skillful writer and at the root of compelling and imaginative metaphor (see Chapter M). Also called cross-sensory metaphors, examples include "loud shirt", "bitter wind", or "prickly laugh".

Sol Stein, author of *Stein on Writing*, uses a good example of switching a sense to heighten the feeling:

> Zalatnick led me into the shop not as if I was a fellow looking for a job but as if I was a friend of a friend. I was sure the men in the shop could smell the difference.

Switching the sense from seeing to smelling, asserts Stein, creates a metaphor that not only describes the feeling in a fresh way but is more powerful and evocative.

Janet Fitch suggests an excellent example of synesthesia: wine reviews. For me this brings to mind the "foxy nose" of a King David Concord, the "crisp laughing notes" of a zinfandel, the "rich buttery bouquet" of a C Blanc du Castel, the "silky rich caramel" and "exotic layers of burnt sugar" of a forty-year-old Taylor Fladgate tawny port.

Psychology & Attitude

How a sense is interpreted by your protagonist

190

relies on her emotional state, memories associated with that sense and her attitude.

Using baby powder as an example, Fitch suggests that you can "describe it literally: sweet, chalky, talcy, dusty, sneezy; or you can use synesthesia: smells pastel, smells tender. Then move to the psychological element. Take an attitude on that smell: insipid, cloying, stultifying, like diaper rash, airless. Try a different attitude: sad, lost, vulnerable, hopeless." You get the picture; we are using a sense-impression based on a memory or emotional experience pinned on that smell to create an entire sensation. What this does, of course, is reveal a great deal about the character in a seamless and powerful way, while establishing a rich setting to the story.

Different Point of View

Again, Fitch provides some good advice on this with the example of how to view objects. She sug-gests "seeing" through the lens of a photo-grapher or the palette of a painter. What this does is several things:

- It evokes the use of different vocabulary, and metaphoric language (always richer than literal description)
- It avoids the static nature of a literal physical description

- It provides additional revelation on character and tone of the scene

Fitch recommends reading books on art for vocabulary. Because light "flows", using it to describe something visually gives motion to the description too. Light moves like water: it "streams across a room"; it "bathes a landscape in russet tones". Light may be described metaphorically as a painter or sculptor: "it strokes, it daubs, it burnishes".

And What About SEX?

First off, a love scene and a sex scene aren't necessarily the same (though they can be). The most poignant love scene can play out without either partner touching. Conversely, a sex scene can take place without any love, such as lust between strangers or a rape. Either way, the writer's responsibility is to describe what is happening from the standpoint of the emotions of the POV characters.

"Editors will tell you," says Sol Stein, "that love scenes are often among the worst-written scenes not only in rejected work but in published work. Such scenes are often mechanical, overly phys-iological, hackneyed, or sentimental."

As with description of any sense, a sex scene must be tied to emotion to work. This even includes a sex scene that isn't a "love scene"; the very absence of emotion on the part of one or both of the characters is a statement the writer is making.

Purely physical description doesn't engage or entice a reader the same way as appealing to their emotions. This is a subject where the tenet "less is more" often applies. Even good erotica, which usually describes sexual activities in detail, uses metaphor rather than physical description to evoke reader response (see below).

Tantalize. Provoke. Use nuance. Be suggestive, rather than descriptive. Be poetic rather than prosaic. Be lyrical and use what you have learned above about describing the senses. Don't be literal; get oblique. Use metaphor, simile, and imagery founded on the protagonist's psyche. For instance, the description of the same sexual act would be different with a stranger than with a long-time mate.

Some of the best sex scenes were written by classic writers like D.H. Laurence. Here's an example from *Lady Chatterley's Lover*:

> *And softly, with that marvelous swoon-like caress of his hand in pure soft desire, softly he stroked the silky slope of her loins, down, down between her soft warm buttocks, coming nearer and nearer to the very quick of her. And she felt him like a flame of desire, yet tender, and she felt herself melting in the flame.*

When writing a sex scene, writers (like lovers) usually find it desirable to linger on the foreplay rather than on the actual sexual act or consummation. It is in the foreplay that the writer can illuminate not just the character herself but the nature of her relationship with her lover. In the scene below from my book *The Cypol* the complexity of Krys's relationship with Cal comes through:

The book snapped shut and his eyes were back on hers, sudden like a thunderstorm. She fought to keep her breaths from convulsing into shallow eddies. "Nothing like the real thing though, is there?" he said in a thick voice. "You want it. I see it in your face."

She found herself focusing on the little space between his two front teeth. He grinned like a pirate and his eyes were dark like a stormy sea, drawing her to him like a drowning sailor even as she thrashed away in a huff. "What part of 'no' don't you understand?"

He smirked and flung the book behind him. " 'No' means 'yes', my rude little peddler."

"*You're* the one who's rude." She glared at him.

"All right, I'm rude," he said and leaned forward, face closing in. The tangy fragrance of orange lingered on his breath. "You're trembling."

"I'm not afraid of you."

"You should be." His lips almost touched hers. "I always get what I want."

"Well, get used to your first disappointment," she said, inhaling the sharp and oily smell of his sweat, and confused by the fact that he was annoying and charming her at the same time. He leaned into her, stirring an ache.

"Don't!" she whispered hoarsely. She was already wet.

"The most essential ingredients in love scenes," says Stein, "are **tension** and **tenderness**."

The sexual act may reveal a great deal about one or both characters through metaphor, imagery, and powerful verbs. Krys's loneliness and general feelings of emptiness and lack of fulfillment in her life are alluded to through the choice of descriptors:

> Mouths joined and slid in a wet embrace. They flung off their clothes and rolled on the musty carpet, the smell of mildew and acrid sweat coiling around her. The ache between her thighs became unbearable. Seizing in sobbing breaths, she clutched at his strong arms and arched into him. He surged inside, filling her with his flesh, and released a gasp from her.
>
> He pounded deep and urgent. With each blow she saw stars. It threw her into another universe. Like a lone raptor she rode the crest of his swells into a brooding darkness.
>
> There, amidst a storm of emotion, he swept her over the edge into a place she'd never known, where her lonely moans joined his in a rising chorus.

195

Sol Stein reminds us that "plot grows out of character. What happens in a love scene should come out of [a] character's...motivation."

Erotica & Erotic Romance

Some writers differentiate between "erotica" and "erotic romance".

Janelle Denison, author of books in the *Harlequin Blaze* and *Temptation* line, defines **straight erotica** as focusing on the sexual aspect of a relationship; scenes contain graphic and explicit sexual scenes intended primarily to stimulate and arouse the reader without necessarily engaging the reader's emotions. She differentiates this from **erotic romance**, which explores an evolving relationship through emotional bonding and the sensuality of the love scenes. She defines erotic romance as "sexual love, and the satisfying of sexual desire with emotional ties between the hero and heroine. Erotic romance is hot and spicy, yet always sensual, bold yet familiar, pushing boundaries yet always making the reader feel as though the hero and heroine are committed to each other in some way—physically and emotionally."

"The main flaw in most love scenes," asserts Stein, "is [that] ... the reader's emotions have been insufficiently considered by the writer. The primary erogenous zone is in the head, and that's where the reader experiences writing."

References

Fitch, Janet. 2000. "Making Sense". In: *Fiction Writer*, April 2000.

Denison, Janelle. 2008. Interview with *Sensual Romance*: http://sensualromance.writerspace.com/jdenisoninterview.html

Hopkin, Michael. 2004. "Link Proved Between Senses and Memory". *BioEd Online*: http://www.bioedonline.org/news/news.cfm?art=985.

Kruszelnicki, Dr. Karl. 1986. *Great Moments in Science: I Don't Believe it!* Chicago Review Pr.

Stein, Sol. 1995. *Stein on Writing*. St. Martin's Griffin. New York. 308pp.

197

T. ❤ Don't Tell; Show

Recently, I attended a crowded workshop entitled "Show don't Tell" given by Robert J. Sawyer at the Surrey International Writers' Conference. Of a certainty, it was packed partly because of Sawyer's dynamic charisma and reputation for accessible instruction. But it was also packed because this is a challenge most writers, whether novice or established, recognize and face daily in their writing. It is something we can all learn to do better.

But What's the Difference, Really?

Let's start with defining "show" as opposed to "tell". Sawyer gave a simple but elegant example during his workshop at SIWC:

>**Telling**:   "I am bald."
>**Showing**:   "The light shone off the
>   top of Rob's head."

In this example, telling is more economical in words, involving only three words to the nine words of showing; however, showing is more evocative, more vivid, more cinematic. And, ultimately, more engaging. This is what showing does; it engages the reader by luring them into the experience of the story. Telling simply imparts information to you without engaging your emotions. Showing, by its very nature, invites you to experience the event being described.

Showing also reveals something about the narrator (usually the main POV character) through their observation.

Dialogue That Shows...or Tells

Dialogue provides an excellent vehicle to show from general description to character motivation and mood (see Chapter D). The reader can learn a great deal about a character from how they speak to what they choose to talk about, which can reveal much about a person's education, philosophy, biases, culture and history. A character's inflections and common vernacular can be used to identify them from a particular region or culture.

Dialogue can also be used to give information about a place, event or idea. However, you need to be mindful not to turn this into a major "info dump". One way to ensure that this does not occur is to make your characters talk to each other, not to the reader. Another is to read your dialogue out loud. Would you—or anyone else—really say *that*? You will also want to pay attention to your dialogue attributes (e.g., the he said, she said part), as these can become quite "telly".

Table 1 looks at various ways of saying the same thing, moving from okay to the best.

Table 1: The Good, Better, Best of Demonstrating

He was in a rage and felt betrayed. "I'm okay, Clara," he said, not meaning it.	**Telling.** Despite the potential for emotional explosion, there is no engagement with the reader; you might as well be reading the newspaper.
He fumed. "I'm okay, Clara," he said caustically.	**Showing.** This is better; the first sentence uses a power verb that conveys the "telling" phrase more succinctly. But, the dialogue attribute uses an adjective, which is typically weak.
He fumed. "I'm okay, Clara." His eyes avoided hers.	**Showing.** Even better. The attribute now describes an emotional response: eye contact, or lack of it, is a powerful tool.

Showing Off Your Body (Language)

How a character stands, walks, or sits shows a great deal about that person's feelings and personality. It also shows us how that character relates to his environment and the other people he is interacting with. Body language is a whole science that most of us aren't even aware that we are using: dilating pupils, blushing skin, nervous tick, etched frown line, crossing one's arms, leaning back in a slouch. All these actions show a great deal without any necessary conscious acknowledgement. I talk a little about this in Chapter D. Faces can be particularly expressive. As a result, an entire science of reading faces—phrenology—has emerged. "There's definitely a connection between the mind and the body," says Barbara Roberts, author of *Face Reading: What Does Your Face Say?* "What you experience spiritually, emotionally and mentally shows up on your face." Forehead, eyebrows, eyelids, cheekbones, eyes, nose, mouth—they all show a great deal.

In a workshop on body language at the Surrey International Writers' Conference several years ago, author Janet Lee Carey recommended that writers learn to: "capture the swift and subtle signals of human communication" and "translate these movements, gestures and facial expressions into written language."

Pay attention to your own body, suggests Carey. "How do you sit? How do you move? How do you breathe?" Pay attention to your moods and what your body does then. For instance, what do you do with your hands when you're nervous? How do you speak when you're impatient? How do you cook when you're happy? How about when you're mad?

Carey lists the areas of the body where emotions can be detected by other characters. These include: skin, breathing, swallowing, eyes, eyebrows, ears, lips, jaw, neck, shoulders, arms, hands, back, sexual organs, legs and feet. On the other hand, physical areas where a character may feel an emotion but not show it are: pain in the body, skin, tongue, throat, heart, stomach, sexual organs, and pulse.

Carey describes several devices in which the writer can use body language imaginatively. These include:

- **Amplification and contradiction:** I describe this in Chapter D, in which body movements and facial expressions either enhance or contradict the verbal expression.

- **Reactions to invasion of personal space**: shown by restlessness, hunching of the shoulders, tucking in of the chin, backing up.

- **Masking**: defending personal space or person by showing indifference or confidence while masking their true feelings (e.g., remember when Luke faced the Emperor in that last battle aboard the Deathstar? Despite his quiet show of confidence, he swallowed—his fear).

Exposition & Info Dumps

Novice writers (and some professionals) often fall into the trap of info dumping instead of presenting information dramatically (i.e., showing it). Unless you're Gabriel García Márquez, who can write superb exposition for pages, the best way is to dramatize your description.

It takes courage and confidence to say less and let the reader figure it out. Exposition needs to be broken up and appear in the right place as part of the story. Story is paramount. Telling is one of the things beginning writers do most and editors will know you for one right away. Think of the story as a journey for both writer and reader. The writer makes a promise to the reader that s/he will provide a rip-roaring story and the reader comes onside, all excited. This is done through a confident tease in the beginning and slow revelation throughout the story to keep it compelling. Exposition needs to be very sparingly used, dealt out in small portions.

Author Elsa Neal gives the following example of showing as opposed to telling in a movie. In it a teenager is trying to find out who her real father is. She doesn't find out herself, Neal tells us, but the audience does—if they are paying attention:

> In one scene quite early in the movie, the teenager orders a cup of tea at a café. She quickly spoons three heaped sugars into the cup and stirs it quite lightly, tapping the spoon on the rim of the cup. She's not really paying attention to what she's doing, but the scene stands out because she's being watched by a boy who's interested in her.
>
> Later, a man is offered a mug of tea together with a bowl of sugar. He heaps three sugars into the mug, stirs lightly, and taps the mug with the spoon. It is so similar to the manner in which the teenager took her tea, that the audience is bound

to be left with an "Aha" moment. This man is her real father.

There is no audience hand-holding, says Neal. The character doesn't make the observation, and therefore doesn't give it to the audience: "Wait a minute. You take three sugars in your tea, just like me. Are you my father?" Instead, the scene itself provides the audience a clue, just as the narrator can in a book. Subtle as a knife.

"It's important to trust your readers to discover the clues you leave when you show part of your story," says Elsa Neal. "When you decide over and over that you must confirm the clues by telling the reader what is going on, you really show the reader that you don't trust her to be intelligent enough to pick up what you mean. And you also show the reader that you don't have enough faith in your own ability as a writer. Let go of some of the control of your story."

Neal provides us with the most important difference between show and tell. Show demonstrates faith in yourself and in your reader.

When is Telling Okay?

Telling has its place in narrative. Telling is very useful when you need to let the reader know about an event or action that you do not want to describe in vivid detail; for instance, a scene that isn't critical. For example:

Sally raced to the airport to catch the

plane.

Simple and succinct telling works effectively as transitional narrative. Instead of spending time with this rather mundane journey through city traffic, we can move forward in a sentence to where the action on the plane—the next critical scene—will occur. Telling sentences serve as bridges for critical showing scenes.

Telling (or exposition) is also useful for revealing back-story and may be the best medium to do this succinctly.

If you are using an unreliable narrator or POV character, telling may be a useful tool to reveal this and keep things otherwise straight for the reader.

When to Tell & When to Show

While we recognize that expository telling has its place and is even desirable in narrative, Sawyer tells us that there is a place and time where exposition works best. This is when both the reader and character needs to know. Sawyer gives the example of a medical practitioner encountering an accident victim who requires an emergency tracheotomy. As he performs his procedure he describes it to his patient because she needs it. Delivered under the best possible

205

conditions (i.e. highest moment of tension), this information becomes critical for both character and reader (who now has a vested interest in knowing the details). This type of exposition seamlessly and dramatically moves the story. The fact that it is done through dialogue is an added bonus.

When you show your work to editors, agents and fellow writers and they describe it as "evocative", "cinematic" or "vivid", take heart—you are showing. If, on the other hand you receive a response that uses the word "padded", you know you've been telling a bit more than you should.

References

Dibell, Ansen. 1999. *Elements of Fiction Writing: Plot*. Writer's Digest Books. Cincinnati, Ohio. 170pp.

Killian, Crawford. 2003. "Show or Tell?". In: *Writing Fiction*: http://crofsblogs.typepad.com/fiction/2003/07/show_or_tell.html

Morrell, David. 2000. "First Blood, Third Person". In: *Fiction Writer*. April, 2000.

Neal, Elsa. 2008. "Showing versus Telling—some examples". In: *Fiction Writing Side* of Bella Online, http://www.bellaonline.com/articles/art47547.asp

Sawyer, Robert J. 2008. "Show Don't Tell". In: *the Surrey International Writers' Conference*, Surrey, B.C., October 23-26, 2008.

U. ● Unclutter Your Writing: Less is More

The K.I.S.S. Principle

"Fiction by new writers often suffers from excessive length," says author Maya Kaathryn Bohnhoff. "Inflated prose is frequently a contributing factor. Too many words are devoted to recounting basic events." She's talking about *telling* versus showing and info-dumping (see Chapter E). Description slows action.

There is a Mennonite adage that applies to writing: "less is more". The KISS principle equally applies. I'm not just talking about language, *per se*, but also storyline,  scene structure, plot, and cast. I'm also not just talking about length, though it is part of the cluttering process. For instance, a short story, by its very shortness, commands simplicity in form, while a novel (particularly if it is part of a trilogy or series) is expected to be more complicated, complex and multi-layered.

One of the best ways to unclutter your writing is to simplify it. "Keep it simple, stupid". This doesn't necessarily mean that you have to be a Spartan and write sparingly like Hemingway. You can use rich language like Jacqueline Carey but apply that language with purpose. While Jacqueline Carey's *Kushiel's Dart* contains rich narrative description, the language is appropriate for the time period and always portrays motion.

The model of achieving "simple" within "complex" is as hard to understand as chaos theory and autopoiesis. So, I won't bother. But I will talk about various writing components that would benefit from simplification.

Sentences & Paragraphs

Fluid writing lies at the basis of uncluttered prose. How do you achieve this? Here are a few suggestions:

1. **Cut down extraneous words:** when constructing a scene, it is wise to pay attention to cadence, rhythm, number of phrases or clauses and general length of sentences. Sentences in early works tend to be full of extra words (e.g., using "ing" verbs, add-ons like "he started to think" instead of simply "he thought") that slow down narrative. Try reading your sen-

tences out loud; this practice often helps you to find the clutter.

2. **Use active & powerful verbs:** in Chapter X, I discuss ways to make your sentences sing by using impeccable language. One of the very best ways to do this is through the use of power-verbs. Active verbs are the key to vivid writing; and, ironically, to uncluttering your writing. Consider, these two paragraphs, which describe the same scene.

   a. Joe walked slowly into the room. His lip curled in disgust as he looked around the room. There were empty beer bottles all over the filthy floor that was covered with stains and garbage and there was a naked couple in the bed. They were almost buried under the rumpled covers. They now struggled to get up and Joe saw the big man staring up at him angrily.

   b. Joe sidled into the room, lip curling at the stench of empty beer bottles and garbage strewn on the stained floor. A naked couple struggled out from the rumple of clothes and blankets. The man reared up and glared at Joe.

   Paragraph a contained sixty-eight words while paragraph b contained only forty-one words. And it's obvious which paragraph sings.

3. **Cut down the words in your paragraphs:** pay particular attention to your intro chapters and cut down your words by at least 20%. Be merciless; you won't miss them, believe me, and you will add others later in your second round of edits. Find the most efficient way to say what you mean. You are guaranteed to achieve this if you follow suggestion number 2.

4. **Reduce redundancy:** a common phenomenon I have found with many writers, including those who write nonfiction, is that the introductory sentence of a narrative paragraph is often paraphrased unnecessarily in the very next sentence; as though the writer didn't trust the reader to get it the first time. Lack of confidence and experience is common with  novice authors and is something that you must learn to combat. Say it once and say it right the first time.

5. **Show, don't tell:** Chapter T discusses why and how to show, not tell. Embracing this way of writing may be the single most effective way to reduce clutter and en-

hance the vividness of your writing at the same time. While showing may in fact add more words than simple telling, the way it is read (mostly in the form of action) makes up for the added words.

Too Many Characters & Too Many Stories

In Chapter C, I talked about the problem of using a "cast of thousands" in your epic fantasy or historical novel—both genres that lend themselves to this. Each character has her quest or journey along with requisite crises and sub-plots. You can see the huge potential for clutter here. In the manuscript with the large cast that I was critiquing, I counted one major magical quest along with several minor quests, intrigue, romance, and several wars. This is all well and good if—and only if—these all integrate well with each other as part of a major theme. If each subplot is a note of one well-constructed melody, then the reader is able to intuitively make her  way through the thicket of characters and subplots. Often, however, this is not the case, and the potential for a reader (and even the writer) to get lost increases dramatically. Essentially, what you end up getting is too many stories (subplots) wrapped inside a larger story.

How do you figure out that a subplot isn't

needed? Much as you can do for a character or any other element of a story, you determine whether the outcome of the story would remain the same if you removed the subplot. If your answer is yes, then it (and sometimes the character carrying it) isn't necessary and is probably just cluttering up your story.

Edgar Allan Poe suggested that if you could pull something out of your story without it collapsing, then that something was probably not necessary to the plot and could even interfere with the reader's comprehension of the story. In all likelihood, the story would thrive better without the unnecessary subplot (and associated extraneous character).

Subplots should contribute more than a clever scene and/or character. "Like the musculature on a skeleton," says Bohnhoff, "they should be integral to the story's movement."

References

Bohnhoff, Maya Kaathryn. 1999. "Taming the Fictional Wilds". In: *Fiction Writer*. April, 1999.

V. ● Voices in Your Head

"Voice" is the feel and tone that applies to the overall book (narrative voice) and to each character. The overall voice is dictated by your audience—youth, adults, crazy people, etc.—as well as the subject matter and general overall theme of the story. "Voice" is also the term used to describe a writer's "voice", the "authorial voice" that is your unique writing style.

Voice creates the look and feel of the story, and ultimately its unique properties. It incorporates the writer's unique voice and any elements she uses for that particular story. Invariably, the voice of the story reflects the author's philosophy, biases and message. What kind of story are you uniquely writing? What is YOUR voice?

Your voice and story is expressed through tone, perspective, style, language and pace. All of these reflect your intent and are ultimately expressed in the story's overarching theme. The overarching theme is ultimately the author's theme, the "world view" of the story. The principal character and minor characters will carry variations on the main theme, each with his or her unique voice.

Narrative Voice

Narrative voice belongs to the persona telling the story. Which persona you adopt in narration depends on what kind of story you are telling, and the kind of emotional atmosphere you wish to achieve, says Crawford Kilian, author of over a dozen novels. The persona develops from the personality and attitude of the narrator, expressed through the narrator's choice of words and depictions.

Character Voice

It's important to give each character a distinctive  "voice" (including use of distinct vernacular, use of specific expressions or phrases, etc.). This is one way a reader can identify a character and find them likeable—or not.

In a manuscript I recently reviewed, I noticed that each character spoke in a mixture of formal and casual speech. This confuses the reader and bumps them out of the fictive dream. Most people's speech is more consistent. Consistency is very important for readers; it helps them identify with a character. They will abandon a story whose writing—and voice—is not consistent. So, my advice to this beginning writer was to pick one style for each character and

214

stick to it. Voice incorporates language (both speech and body movements), philosophy, and humor. How a character looks, walks, talks, laughs, is all part of this. Let's take laughter for instance: does your character tend to giggle, titter, chortle, guffaw, belly laugh? Does she usually put her hand over her mouth when she does? Does she do or say certain things when she's nervous? (see also Chapter C and D).

Whose Viewpoint Is It, Anyway?

The story's viewpoint can be told from several perspectives and which one you choose can be critical to how your story comes across. Different stories lend themselves to different narrative styles and points of view (POVs). David Morrell, author of *First Blood*, warns that some writers may "select a viewpoint merely because it feels natural, but if you...don't consider the implications of your choice...your story might fight you until you abandon it, blaming the plot when actually the problem is how you're telling it." (*Fiction Writer*, April 2000).

The choices are several:
- omniscient
- third person limited
- first person
- second person

Omniscient Viewpoint

The **omniscient view** is the broadest view. The narrator is essentially "God" describing everything and everyone and dropping into any character at any time, as if by whimsy at times—and in the case of a beginning writer—all too confusingly in the same paragraph. The omniscient narrator may step back and describe societies or historical events like a journalist or historian with characters being generally unaware. Many of the classics are written in this style. In *Tale of Two Cities*, Charles Dickens fills all of Chapter One with omniscient philosophy (something most writing classes these days warn against).

While this POV is the easiest one to use (like a default) it is really the hardest to master, particularly for today's multiplex reader. In the wrong hands, this viewpoint can be as intrusive as it is distancing. Ironically, many first manuscripts often start in the omniscient POV (that of the narrator) and ever so often lapse into several characters' POV briefly. This makes for very "telling vs. showing" type of writing. Ninety  percent of writers do not write this way because it tends to be off-putting, it distances the reader from the characters, and is hard to maintain consistency. The omniscient viewpoint is considered archaic, and is prone to promoting polemic (particularly in the hands of a beginner); as a result, the novel may quickly evolve from story to dissertation. While there may be a place for this type of narrative, be aware that by choosing to write a treatise, you are limiting your audience (to those who agree with your polemic).

In the hands of a masterful writer, this viewpoint

can make for the most powerful and rich storytelling. Epics of any kind, especially epic fantasies or historical epics, lend themselves to this style. The omniscient viewpoint is particularly suited to a story that is large, where ultimately the main character is not any particular protagonist but the story itself, or a society or a world or time period. The writer must still somehow achieve connection and intimacy with the reader to succeed with this viewpoint. Masterful writers do this through lyrical and compelling narrative, poetic language and powerful imagery. They draw the reader into their world despite one's distance from the characters. They accomplish this by providing the reader with a substitute: the grandeur and scope of the story itself and the universal truth associated with it. One writer who does this with impeccable style is Thomas Hardy. Using rich metaphor and vivid imagery, Hardy paints a world both compelling and engrossing:

> *Amid the oozing fatness and warm ferments of Frome Vale, at the season when the rush of juices could almost be heard below the hiss of fertilization, it was impossible that the most fanciful love should not grow passionate. The ready hearts existing there were impregnated by their surroundings.*
> —Tess of the d'Urbervilles

Limited Third Person Viewpoint

Most writers prefer to use **limited third person** POV (told by one or a few key characters; that is, you get into the head and thoughts of only a

217

few people: all the observations are told through their observations, what they see, feel and think). This bonds the reader to your characters and makes for much more compelling reading. I would highly suggest you adopt this style, particularly if you are starting out. That's not to say that you can't use several POVs... just not at the same time (e.g., in the same paragraph or scene); it is the norm to use chapter or section breaks to change a POV.

The use of limited third person is...limitless (sorry for the awful pun). So long as you respect the reader's need for clarity by keeping to one POV per scene, you can choose to enter into the heads of as many characters as you wish. In Margorie B. Kellogg's *The Book of Water* of her *Dragon Quartet*, the POV  effectively shifts between chapters from the past-tense third person of the young girl, Erde, to the present-tense third person of N'doch. David Morrell shares in *Fiction Writer* (April 2000) how he "reju-venated" his book, *First Blood*, by shifting POVs between the antagonist, Wilfred Teasle, and the protagonist, Rambo. Both writers very carefully selected whose POV to use in a particular scene. Through whose eyes will the reader best view the scene or circumstance?

In the section of my book, *The Last Summoner*, where the young medieval Prussian baroness, Vivianne, is thrown into modern-day Paris, I chose to shift from her POV to the eyes of the

Parisian François who discovers her. For me—and presumably the reader—telling it through the native as opposed to the disoriented visitor was far more entertaining. It also gave me the chance to describe the main character, out of her element, through the eyes of one who was not. In *Defining Diana*, a science fiction mystery, Hayden Trenholm shifts from the first person perspective of Police Superintendent Frank Steele to the third person viewpoint for his remaining characters. This particular combination proves very effective in both creating variety for the reader and highlighting the most important character. It also manages to maintain the familiar trope of first person for detective mystery while adding a refreshing element to it.

Second Person Viewpoint

The **second person viewpoint** ("you") is not often used. There is a reason for this; it is both distancing and less easy to read; it is hard for readers to embrace and can be rather off-putting. So, why do it? Again, this depends on the story being told. If you wish to purposefully impart a distance to the narrator, due to their own limitations or an infirmity, then this view could work well. It is usually limited to more eclectic and artistic stories and is hard to read in a long form, like a novel. I chose to tell one of my short stories in this viewpoint because the narrator was psychologically troubled, had a problem with the subject matter being narrated, and I thought it fit with the tone. I later reframed the story in the first person and I think it worked better. But I still like the second-person version for its slightly disturbing tone.

219

You scour the chaos for those fragments of memory, taped together by longing, and see her as she once was, as she always was. She was just your cousin, but when you were still children, she killed for you. Slew a man who charged at you with a knife, the one he'd used to kill your parents. When your brother was attacked and cried out, she flew to his aid and threw herself into a den of assault.

Then, when she pleaded for your help, you ran.

It was the revolution, you say. You were just a boy, only ten years old. You know better. The revolution defined what you are. She faced fear head on, bravely pushed it aside and rose like an angel to the call. You let fear chase you to the depths of infinity.

You wander infinity's dark shores, stranded in that moment of agony, still hearing her screams and aching to fly.

— Butterfly in Peking

First Person Viewpoint

The **first person viewpoint** is both the most limiting perspective (told only through one viewpoint) and most revealing—of that viewpoint character.

The writer needs to decide how reliable the POV character is in telling the story and how to impart this to the reader. There is only so far a writer can go with an unreliable viewpoint character before losing their own credibility and the reader in the long run. Obviously a balance is required.

Who Should Tell the Story?

When telling a story through the eyes of a single viewpoint character, it makes most sense to tell it through the main character, the protagonist, around whom the story usually revolves. She is the one who's going to be chiefly affected by the events of the story. Ansen Dibell, author of *The Elements of Fiction: Plot*, asks the question: "Who is really at the story's heart?" If you're having trouble with the story of Sally and Norman from Sally's point of view, perhaps you

should try telling it through Norman's point of view. Or perhaps your main POV character is a third per-son, looking on and, in turn, changed.

Narrating a story from an outsider's viewpoint (the hidden protagonist as observer-narrator)— sometimes called displaced narrative—can also add an element of complexity and depth to a story. *The Illusionist* is a good example of this. This story, about Eisenheim (the Illusionist) and his beloved, is told through the cynical eyes of the city's chief inspector, who learns to believe again through his "experience" of their story. Other examples include J.P. Hartley's *The Go-Between*, Scott Fitzgerald's *The Great Gatsby*, *Saving Private Ryan*, *My Beloved*, Charlotte Bronte's *Wuthering Heights*, and Joanne Harris's *Chocolat*.

Using a displaced viewpoint character to narrate a story works particularly well if you want to keep your main character strange and mysterious. Having an outside character tell the story of one or two other characters also gives the writer a chance to add another thematic element to a story (the one belonging to the narrator). A story told through the eyes of a dreamer will be very different than one told by a ponderous thinker.

Other kinds of narration include:

- **detached autobiography** (narrator looks back on long-past events; e.g., *To Kill a Mockingbird* by Harper Lee)

- **letters or diary** (narrative told through letters, also known as the epistolary novel; e.g. my short story, *Arc of Time*)

- **interior monologue** (narrator recounts the story as a memory; stream of consciousness is an extreme form of this narrative, e.g., *Ulysses* by James Joyce)

How Many Should Tell the Story?

The use of multiple viewpoints is common among writers and adds an element of richness and breadth to a story. With each added character's POV, readers are more enlightened to the thoughts and motivations of characters in a story. When you have several characters telling the story, this is called a rotating viewpoint. A few points to follow include:

- Alternate or rotate your differing viewpoints clearly (scene by scene, chapter by chapter, or part by part)
- **Don't** change viewpoints **within a scene**
- Separate different POV scenes within chapters with extra white space or some kind of graphic (e.g., ****)

References

Dibell, Ansen. 1999. *Elements of Fiction Writing: Plot.* Writer's Digest Books. Cincinnati, Ohio. 170pp.

Kilian, Crawford. 2003. "Narrative Voice". In: *Writing Fiction*: http://crofsblogs.typepad.com/fiction/2003/07/narrative_voice.html

Morrell, David. 2000. "First Blood, Third Person". In: *Fiction Writer.* April, 2000.

W. • Who, Where, When and Why of Doing Research

To Research or Not to Research...

Research is something many writers dislike and find daunting or even intimidating. In truth, as a writer, you are doing research all the time: when you're riding the bus or train to work, when you're traveling on vacation, when you're having a lively discussion—or better yet an argument—with a friend or colleague. Everything you experience and observe is research. This is what I call non-directed research. It's also called living. Writers, like all artists, are reporters of life, actively participating and passively observing. A writer is an opportunist, gathering her data through her daily life experiences.

...That is the Question...

You might be saying: well, that's all well and good for a historical-mystery set in Budapest or a science fiction thriller set in the Vega system. But you don't need to do research because you're writing a fantasy or a memoir. Neither of these, on the face of it, appears to require research: the fantasy is based on a totally made up world, after all, and the memoir is all about you. So, why bother? As a matter of fact, they both need research. Most books do, particularly nowadays for our multiplex, intelligent and discerning readership. I mentioned this already in Chapter A about world building; readers of any fiction enjoy learning something when they read, particularly when it's seamless and made easy through a compelling story. It's a real bonus.

To return to the fantasy, you will find very quickly that in order to build a consistent world (even if it's mostly from your own imagination), you will need to draw upon something real to anchor your imaginary world upon. Whether this reflects a powerful myth or forms an alternative version of a real society, you will still need to apply some rules to follow, so you don't lose your reader.

With respect to the memoir, the need for research lies in placing your story in context with some event, idea, theme or place of interest to attract readership. Unless you're a world unto yourself (e.g., you're a celebrity of some kind with an established following), your story will require this larger element within which to place your personal story. That's where research comes in. See?

...Whether 'Tis Nobler in the Mind...

Research for your book or short story will take on many forms from subtle to obvious and from non-directed (opportunistic) to directed (e.g., library). What form your research takes on and how rigorous it is will vary according to your purpose and circumstance. And where you go to do your research will vary accordingly. It's really a bit of a mind game. I do research all the time in my work as a scientist. You could almost call it my middle name (Nina *Research* Munteanu).

...To Suffer the Slings & Arrows...

What I've found, even in my work in the traditional field of hard science, is that we have all gone digital. The chances are that your favorite newspaper or magazine has a strong online presence. The Internet provides an excellent platform for finding resources in a myriad subjects. It is the largest single place where you can find current information relevant to almost anything.

I stress current because this has been one of the challenges in some areas of research. Medical research is a good example. The professor of one of my fourth-year physiology courses announced to his class on our first day that he had scrapped the textbook (which he claimed was already dated by the time it was published) in preference of more current scientific papers from conferences and symposia. His point was that the printing process takes time and in the meantime research marches on. This is where the Internet is so powerful.

With information so readily accessible and easy to find through Google and other search engines as well as giant amoeba-like encyclopedia wiki sites such as Wikipedia, you needn't suffer those arrows of frustrating library and book searches (though I still find this kind of research ultimately satisfying—so long as I have time). And there is risk...

...Of Outrageous Science...

I talked a little about scientific research in Chapter A, on the world-building section. The subgenre I often write for is Hard Science Fiction. This group of readers is very well-read and know their science. They fully expect your research of current science to be impeccable and accurate and your premise (based on that science) to be a realistic projection. In science fiction, particularly hard science fiction, science is a critical part of the story. Most idea-driven stories, such as those by Robert J. Sawyer, Greg Bear, Michael Crichton, and William Gibson explore the what ifs with wonderfully enlightening extrapolations of societal, environmental and scientific consequences.

Having said that, you don't need to be a scientist to write this sort of stuff. Neither Robert J. Sawyer nor Greg Bear have particularly strong science backgrounds. However, science background aside, both these acclaimed authors sure know how to do research.

Or to Take Arms Against a Sea of Research

The risk I referred to in the last section is related ironically to the very accessibility of online information. You need to be even more vigilant of the veracity and reliability of your sources when conducting online research. Everyone and their dog is out there, after all. I should know. I am one of them, as no doubt you are. My blog, *The Alien Next Door*, which entertains several thousands of readers a week who like to read my posts on science, pop culture, and writing, is a repository of information. Being a scientist of some repute, I research my articles and often provide proof in the form of citations and a reference list. When doing research, particularly on the Internet (but anywhere), you should do several things:

- Use more than one source, particularly for important things; this will give you a wider range of material from which to discern accuracy and reliability.
- Verify your sources and preferably cross-reference to measure out objective "truth" versus bias.
- Try to use primary sources (original) vs. secondary or tertiary sources (original cited and open to interpretation); the closer you are to the original source, the closer you are to getting the original story.
- When going to more than one source, try to get a range of different source-types (e.g., conservative newspaper versus blog versus special interest site, etc.) to gain a full range of insight into the issue you're researching.

...And by Opposing End Them?

Don't forget that highly valuable and satisfying

research can take on the form of interview. You can gain incredible insight into the subject of your research by using a live expert. The advantages he or she has to a book or online database is that they interact with you and may give you something you didn't even know you needed. Experts exist everywhere and are, for the most part, usually amenable to interview. So long as you are respectful and don't take up too much of their time, I find that most people are rather intrigued when I tell them that they are helping me with some research I'm conducting for the book I'm writing. I usually promise a copy of the book to them, once it's published.

Experts include people in your community, your neighbors and friends, professionals in business and in the universities and other educational facilities. Special interest forums and sites can be used to access people to interview.

Perchance to Dream...

I've spent some time discussing directed research with you. What about non-directed research? The stuff of which dreams are made. By its very nature, non-directed research is less information than knowledge. This is the deep stuff, the mortar that fills in the bricks that you've laid through your directed research. It's the so what part. And that is more intuitively gained.

...For in that Sleep...

Early on in my writing career, I started carrying a notebook with me wherever I went. I kept notepads in all my jacket pockets, stuffed them into the glove box of my car. I even trained my friends to carry notepaper and pens on them through my frequent requests.

I found that, while I was working on a story, events and opportunities presented themselves that were directly relevant to my project. It was serendipity in action. That, and the fact that my mind was focused on anything to do with my current piece. It was as though I had donned a concentrating filter, one that would amplify relevant details. I'll venture even further; I was unconsciously acting in a way that would bring me more information relevant to my project. So, the notebook was very handy indeed. It was my talisman. And a vehicle to my imaginary world.

One thing I haven't learned to do is organize my notebooks by some logical means. As a result, my scattered thoughts have remained just that: scattered throughout my three dozen or so notebooks. Oops! If you can come up with a logical way of filing your notebooks, let me know.

Okay, there's another version of a "notebook"; which includes small laptops, palmtops, BlackBerries, even some cell phones. All these digital devices are capable of recording and storing your thoughts and observations. If you've embraced them, use them. The point is that you have some means at your disposal to record your thoughts as they come to you, wherever you may be.

...What Dreams May Come...

I keep a journal or scrapbook for every novel I write. This permits me to do several things:

1. Organize relevant research material into one place for easy access (which makes up for my appalling note taking practices).

2. Satisfy my inclination for info dump and expository back-story by providing a place to house it—in my journal, where it belongs, instead of in the story.

By the time I was through with it, the journal I'd kept of my last book—a historical fantasy set in medieval Prussia and modern-day Paris—was its own rich compendium of interesting information, lovingly put together with photos of Paris, drawings and sketches of castles, armor, and long swords, maps of great battles, spreadsheets of timelines and family trees and, of course, commentary on all the great cafés and patisseries in Paris between Rue Princess and Boulevard Saint-Michel.

X. ● Use eXceptional Language ...but Don't Overdo it

It took me fifteen years to discover I had no talent for writing, but I couldn't give it up because by that time I was too famous
—Robert Benchley

Moving From Prosaic to Spectacular

What makes some writing stunning and other writing lackluster? Mostly, it's the language—the words—you use. And, it isn't just *what* words you use; it's *how* you use them. Here are a few things you need to consider when translating your work into something that sings.

Use active verbs and reduce modifiers: many writers, not just beginners, slide into the pattern of using passive and weak verbs (e.g., were, was, being, etc.). Then they add a modifier to strengthen it. It doesn't. Actively look for strong, vivid verbs. This is a key to good writing. I can't emphasize this enough. For instance, which version is more compelling?

> Jill **was walking quickly** into the room.
> or…
> Jill **stormed** into the room.

Avoid using excessive prose: novice writers often use too many words to describe an event, action or scene. An overabundance of words slows down the story and obscures plot and action. In Chapter U, I discuss how to pare down your prose to make it more vivid. When you look for a more efficient way to say something you cut out unnecessary detail. Using active verbs and avoiding modifiers helps greatly, like the above example.

Use alliteration, metaphor, simile, personification (but don't overuse): these devices bring lyricism and cadence and powerful imagery to your prose. However, as with anything powerful, you need to use these judiciously. Use them where you wish to convey a strong image and to punctuate your prose.

Be mindful of word-accuracy: more often than you might think, a writer inadvertently misuses a word to convey an idea or emotion. For instance, let's consider the following sentence, which describes a character's reaction to a dog being cruelly mishandled:

> "What are they doing?" Reginald said crossly.

The modifier *crossly* suggests that Reginald lacks compassion; it implies petulant annoyance.

> "What are they doing?" Reginald scowled.

This suggests the same icy disdain as the above quote.

On the other hand, if the writer wished to convey shock, disgust or compassion, the following would better represent that sentiment:

> "What are they doing?" Reginald said, eyes wide.

Or:

> "What are they doing?" Reginald stammered.

Avoid using words like "felt" or "seem": these "telly" words prevent the reader from directly experiencing the story by imposing a level of interpretation. For example, "he felt himself falling" can be improved to "he fell". If you want to spice up the phrase, use another verb: "he toppled" "he stumbled" or "he crashed".

Read your writing aloud & punctuate your pauses: it isn't just a clever metaphor that your writing style is called your voice; because your readers listen to what you write. Reading out loud helps define cadence, tone and pace of your prose and streamlines your writing. When you read aloud, pay attention to where you naturally pause. You may wish to put in a comma, semi-colon or period there.

Size your paragraphs: paragraphs are visual elements that help people read; they break up text on a page in logical places to provide white space for reader ease. I've heard people quote the two-inch rule for maximum paragraph length and I concur. This is one of the reasons some passages are harder to read than others; long paragraphs are more tiring to the eye. Find those logical breaks and put them in.

Size your sentences: as with paragraphs, overly long sentences can try a reader's patience and you may lose them entirely. Too many short choppy sentences can also reduce your prose to a mundane level. Varying your sentence length in a paragraph creates the lyricism and cadence that makes prose enjoyable to read.

He Said, She Said...

In Chapter D, I discuss the use of dialogue tags and the common misconception that the word said is overused, overrated and downright boring. "The truth is," says Maya Kaathryn Bohnhoff, author of *The Crystal Rose*, "*said* is not boring unless the ideas, action and dialogue around it are boring." You are better off improving your dialogue, writing more vivid scenes with compelling characters than searching for better ways to say said.

Common Grammar Mistakes We All Make

The Mississippi State University Electrical and Computer Engineering Department posted a comprehensive page on the most common grammatical errors North Americans make. These include:

Apostrophe misuse	Misused semicolons
Article errors	Mixed construction
Awkward phrasing or idiom	Parallelism
Capitalization errors	Past tense errors
Comma omissions and	Plurality errors (nouns)

splicing

Contractions	Pronoun case errors, ambiguous and redundant, reference
Double negatives	Shifts in person or number
Faulty coordination	Shifts in tense
Fragments	Subject-verb agreement
Fused or run-on sentences	Unnecessary commas
Misplaced or dangling modifiers	Verb errors (wrong form)

I'm not going to focus a lot on grammar with you, mainly because I'm not the best grammarian (I met my marketing manager when she corrected the spelling on my blog!). Instead, I direct you to these following exceptional guides for writing style and grammar and urge you to adopt one and keep it by your side (my personal favorite is Strunk and White, not just because it's small but because it packs a lot inside):

- Bernstein, Theodore M. 1977. *The Careful Writer: A Modern Guide to English Usage*. Atheneum. New York. 487pp.

- Fowler, H.W. 1983. *The Dictionary of Modern English Usage*. Oxford University Press. 2nd Edition.748pp.

- O'Maolmhuire, Mary. 2004. *Watch Your Language*. 2nd edition. Gill and Macmillan.

- Strunk, William Jr. and E.B. White. 1979. *Elements of Style*. McMillan Publishing Co., Inc. New York. 85pp.

- Online: *The UVic's Writing Guide: Knowing the Basics of Grammar*. http://web.uvic.ca/wguide/Pages/GrammarToc.html

- Online: Lynch, Jack. *A Guide to Grammar and Style*. http://andromeda.rutgers.edu/~jlynch/Writing/

My own weakness in grammar aside, I've included in Table 1 some of the most common structural errors I've noticed in the manuscripts I've critiqued.

Table 1: Common Sentence Structure Errors

Misplaced modifier:	*Put the modifier as close as possible to the noun it is modifying.* **Wrong**: I urge you to cease dumping waste into streams that kills fish. **Fixed**: I urge you to cease dumping waste that kills fish into streams.
Dangling (or misplaced) participle:	*Refer the participial phrase at the beginning of a sentence to the grammatical subject of the sentence.* **Wrong**: As the largest reptiles to have lived, small mammals could not compete with dinosaurs. **Fixed**: Small mammals could not compete with dinosaurs, the largest reptiles to have lived. **Wrong**: Using a hydrolab, the turbidity was measured. **Fixed**: Using a hydrolab, he measured the turbidity.
Fragment	*Unless you are doing this for effect (as in, breaking the rules for emphasis) you need to include a subject and a verb.* **Fragment**: To understand the use of a hydrolab. **Sentence**: To understand the use of a hydrolab he studied the instructions.
Fused sentence:	*Also known as run-on sentence. Break it into two or more sentences and insert commas between clauses.*

	Wrong: The hydrolab is used to measure water quality parameters it is most often used to measure temperature and dissolved oxygen with depth. **Right**: The hydrolab is used to measure water quality parameters. It is most often used to measure temperature and dissolved oxygen with depth.
Parallelism:	*Words or ideas in a sentence that are parallel in meaning must be parallel in structure as well.* **Wrong**: Seeing is to believe. **Right**: Seeing is believing.
Shifting Tenses:	*Keep the tense consistent within a sentence and paragraph.* **Wrong**: Jack went to the game and leaves early. **Right**: Jack went to the game and left early.

It's those pesky irregular verbs that particularly give writers problems. Here are a few examples of particularly troublesome ones, which we often confuse and get mixed up. Their forms are listed in order of present, past, past participle and present participle:

- Lay, laid, laid, laying
- Lie, lay, lain, lying
- Rise, rose, risen, rising
- Stink, stank, stunk, stinking

The first two verbs, lay and lie, are often confused and misused. Lie means to recline, whereas lay means to put something down.

238

Another way to see it is that "lie" is when someone does something to himself or herself; "lay" means that the subject is acting on something or someone else (e.g., she lay the book down on the table before lying down for a nap.)

Common Misspellings

Some common misspellings that come across editors' desks appear below:

A Short List of Common Misspellings

Wrong	Right
todo	to do
allways,	always
upto	up to
allright	all right
theirselves	themselves
pronounciation	pronunciation
explaination	explanation
definately	definitely

A few very common words that many writers mix up include:

- **"Everyday"** (adjective that means common, ordinary); **"every day"** (two word adverbial phrase that means "daily")

- **"There"** (refers to a place "let's go there" or as a pronoun "there is a dream); **"their"** (possessive adjective; "she drove their car"); **"they're"** (contraction for "they are")

239

- "To" (as in to do); "too" (as in too much); "two" (as in two dollars)

- "Affect" (verb); "effect" (noun): e.g., you affect an effect.

Apostrophes & Other Kinky Things

Apostrophes serve two purposes: 1) to indicate possession, and 2) to create a contraction. The most common mistakes are in the use of:

- "its" (possessive adjective; e.g., "go about its business") versus "it's" (contraction for "it is")

-

- "whose" (possessive adjective) versus "who's" (contraction for "who is")

- "lets" (e.g., "he lets his dog run") versus "let's" (contraction for "let us")

- "Your" (possessive adjective; e.g., "please give me your book") versus "you're" (contraction for "you are").

An apostrophe plus an 's' does not make a noun plural. But it does indicate the possessive. What I mean is... well, here is an example: the punctuation of one sentence is "the sentence's punctuation"; the punctuation of several sentences is "the sentences' punctuation".

Why Writers Can't Spell

When I participated in those humiliating spelling

bees in primary school, I was usually among the last chosen because I was a lousy speller. I grew up in an immigrant family where Romanian was the official language; I heard my parents speaking German in the house and lived in a French-Canadian neighborhood. English was actually the fourth language I learned and only once I started going to school. It seemed that my facility with language came at some expense. My spelling sucked. It didn't help that I was probably borderline ADD, dyslexic and allergic to reading.

Are you a lousy speller too? Well, take heart. You're in excellent company. Samuel R. Delany is dyslexic. Thomas Jefferson, F. Scott Fitzgerald, Herman Melville, Woodrow Wilson and John Irving were all rotten spellers.

SF/F writer, Tobias Buckell, author of *Sly Mongoose*, says that "homophones practically kill me, even the ones I know are wrong, b, d, g, and p are often swapped, as is, of course, 6 and 9." He confesses that rewriting "is a painful, deliberate struggle" as he must pore over his work word by word.

So, why is it that some of us can just look at the word "preposterous" and spell it, while others can see it a thousand times and never get it right? Neuroscience has shown us that it's in the brain. Recent studies using functional MRI analysis have not only begun to map the areas of the brain we use in reading and writing, they've shown how a neurological glitch in about twenty percent of people may make them chronically poor spellers.

My particular weakness is the homonym. These are words that sound the same but are spelled differently (e.g., right and write). I've seen writers mix homonyms a lot in my workshops and manuscript critiques. Common ones include:

There, their, they're	Bare, bear
To, too, two	Grate, great
Who's, whose	Here, hear
Reel, real	Meet, meat
Deer, dear	Heel, heal
Brake, break	Council, counsel
Mantle, mantel	Principle, principal
Which, witch	Where, wear

Keep a dictionary by your side and consult it often. For those of you, like me, who spend most of your writing time in front of the computer with Internet access, you may wish to bookmark the online Merriam-Webster dictionary, www.m-w.com.

If you are, like Tobias Buckell, particularly susceptible to self-correcting when you revise your work, then have someone you trust proofread for you.

References

Bernstein, Theodore M. 1977. *The Careful Writer: A Modern Guide to English Usage.* Atheneum. New York. 487pp.

Bohnhoff, Maya Kaathryn. 1999. "Taming the Fictional Wilds". In: *Fiction Writer.* April, 1999.

Fowler, H.W. 1983. *The Dictionary of Modern English Usage.* Oxford University Press. 2nd Edition.748pp.

Hendrix, Steve. 2005. "Why Stevie Can't Spell. In: The Washington Post, February 20, 2005. http://www.washingtonpost.com/ac2/wp-dyn/A27074-2005Feb15?language=printer

Lynch, Jack. *A Guide to Grammar and Style.* http://andromeda.rutgers.edu/~jlynch/Writing/

Mississippi State University. Bagley College of Engineering. http://www.ece.msstate.edu/academics/writing_resource/grammatical_errors.html

O'Maolmhuire, Mary. 2004. *Watch Your Language.* 2nd edition. Gill and Macmillan.

Strunk, William Jr. and E.B. White. 1979. *Elements of Style.* McMillan Publishing Co., Inc. New York. 85pp.

University of Victoria. *The Uvic's Writing Guide: Knowing the Basics of Grammar.* http://web.uvic.ca/wguide/Pages/GrammarToc.html

Y. ● Yesterday, Today, and Tomorrow...

> *It was the best of times, it was the worst of times*
> —Charles Dickens, *A Tale of Two Cities*

Choosing your Tense...

Have you taken the time to consider tense in your story? While most stories are told in the past tense (e.g., Vinnie ran out of the house), I've seen many written in the present tense (e.g., Vinnie runs out of the house). You see the latter more in literary and esoteric works, where the immediacy and dream-like quality of present tense is in keeping with the kind of story being told.

I write mostly genre fiction (e.g., science fiction, SF thrillers, historical fantasy, etc.) where the story-telling is normally fast-paced. These read much better in the past tense. Stories which follow a more reflective tone can be quite powerful in the present tense. Some genre stories may even fall into this category. I chose to write the dream sequences in my novel *Darwin's Paradox* in the present tense.

> *Julie walks SAM's crystal matrix, gazing at the shimmering of purple and*

244

green logic along the passageways. She imagines herself a creature of coloured light, a pilgrim like Dante, who wanders SAM's vast and ordered landscape in search of home. SAM used to "live" in her head back in Icaria. Her AI partner, her best friend. This must be a dream then, she thinks.
  —Darwin's Paradox

In this example, the dark reflective nature of the subject matter and the narrator fits well with present tense.

In her series *The Dragon Quartet*, Marjorie B. Kellogg alternates from past tense to present tense as she hops from one protagonist's point of view to the other's. This deliberate shift in tense between sections works very well. The key is that she is consistent.

...And Keeping It

In the manuscripts that I read for novice writers I often find what I call uncontrolled shifting of tense within a sentence or paragraph. Here's an example from the University of Purdue Online Writing Lab, OWL:

> "The ocean **contains** rich minerals that **washed down** from rivers and streams."

Contains is present tense, referring to a current state; *washed down* is past, but should be present (*wash down*) because the minerals are still washing down.

Corrected: "The ocean **contains** rich minerals that **wash down** from rivers and streams."

Keep the tense of your verbs consistent within a sentence, unless the second action takes place in an earlier time frame (e.g., Jack **loves** the house that Jill **built** for him). Shifting tenses within a sentence or paragraph is okay so long as you know what you're doing.

Shifting Tenses—It Wasn't My Fault, Officer!

Author Elsa Neal suggests that writers inadvertently shift tenses because they mix up dialogue (usually in the present tense) with narrative (usually in the past tense). She adds that some of us have a tendency to describe (in dialogue) past events in the present tense: "So, I order the fish, and it arrives, and it's still got the head on, and I absolutely freak."

OWL provides these hints:

- Use past tense to narrate events and to refer to ideas as historical entities.

- Use present tense to state facts, to refer to perpetual or habitual actions, and to discuss your own ideas or those expressed by an author in a particular work; also to describe action in a literary work, movie, or other fictional narrative.

- Future action may be expressed in a variety of ways, including the use of *will, shall, is going to, are about to, tomorrow*

246

and other adverbs of time, and a wide range of contextual cues.

Let's Progress from Simple to Perfect

Past tense verbs exist as simple, perfect and progressive. Here is a simple past narration with perfect and progressive elements:

> By the time Jane *noticed* the doorbell, it *had* already *rung* three times. As usual, she *had been listening* to loud music on her iPod. She *turned* the iPod *down* and *stood up* to answer the door. A young man *was standing* on the steps. He *began* to speak slowly, asking for directions.

Here it is as simple present with those perfect progressive elements:

> By the time Jane *notices* the doorbell, it *has* already *rung* three times. As usual, she *has been listening* to loud music on iPod. She *turns* the iPod *down* and *stands up* to answer the door. A young man *is standing* on the steps. He *begins* to speak slowly, asking for directions.

And here it is in future narration:

> By the time Jane *notices* the doorbell, it *will have* already *rung* three times. As usual, she *will have been listening* to loud music on her iPod. She *will turn* the iPod *down* and *will stand up* to answer the door. A young man *will be standing*

on the steps. He *will begin* to speak slowly, asking for directions.

The Perfect Tense

According to OWL, the perfect tense is determined by its relationship to the tense of the primary narration. "If the primary narration is in simple past, then action initiated before the time frame of the primary narration is described in past perfect. If the primary narration is in simple present, then action initiated before the time frame of the primary narration is described in present perfect. If the primary narration is in simple future, then action initiated before the time frame of the primary narration is described in future perfect." Clear as mud, right? Okay, here's an example:

- By the time Nina *finished* (past) talking, everyone *had finished* (past perfect) their dinner.

- By the time Nina *finishes* (present: habitual action) talking, everyone *has finished* (present perfect) their dinner.

- By the time Nina *finishes* (present: suggesting future time) talking, everyone *will have finished* (future perfect) their dinner.

Time-orienting words and phrases like *before, after, by the time*—when used to relate two or more actions in time—are good indicators of the need for a perfect-tense verb in a sentence, says OWL.

Don't Get Tense—Do Something About it!

The main tense in the example below is past. Tense shifts (shown in **bold**) are inappropriate:

> Kathryn blushed. She appraised Jake's showman's eyes, his firm jaw and the loose smile he always wore. Her gaze traced his seamless brow, partially hidden beneath thick curls of chestnut hair. Yes, he **is** a knock out. She **rises** from her seat to greet him.

Is should be *was*, and *rises* should be *rose*. This kind of inappropriate shift from past to present is common with novice writing and hard to resist. This is because the writer was drawn into the narrative and began to relive the event.

The main tense in the following example is present. Tense shifts—all appropriate—are indicated in **bold**.

> His eyes sweep down his deformed and gnarled body. Angry scars encrust his livid hairless skin. He remembers colliding two days ago with her and her hand unintentionally **brushed** his thigh. She **jerked** back, blushing with the shame of not knowing how to avoid staring at him in revulsion. Then she **rushed** off before he could speak. Probably to the bathroom to wash her hand, he decides. She **will be telling** "monster" stories to her girlfriends. They **will laugh** and groan and steal a sideways glance at him then giggle.

I use the present tense to describe the appearance of the protagonist. However, both past and future tenses are called for when he refers to Kathryn's previous actions and to her predictable activity in the future.

What About Flashbacks?

Lengthy flashback scenes would become tiresome if they stayed in perfect past tense (e.g., Jill **had said** to Jack). Authors usually use that tense in the beginning of the flashback, just to establish the past, then move back to simple past, understanding that the reader will stay there with them.

References

OWL. 2004. University of Purdue Online Writing Lab. http://owl.english.purdue.edu/handouts/grammar

Neal, Elsa. 2008. "Past and Present Tense." In: Fiction Writing Site of BellaOnline, http://www.bellaonline.com/articles/art51567.asp

2. ❂ The Zen of Passionate Writing

Are you afraid to write, to answer the call of your creative urges? Good. If you're not scared, you're not writing.
   —Ralph Keyes

Everyone deserves to be who they are
   —Tigre Milena

"Being creative means giving yourself the freedom to be who you really are," says Nancy Slonim Aronie, author of *Writing from the Heart: Tapping the Power of Your Inner Voice.*

But that takes courage. A lot of courage.

Finding the Courage to Write

Ralph Keyes, author of *The Courage to Write*, admits that "what makes writing so scary is the perpetual vulnerability of the writer. It's not the writing as such that provokes our fear so much as other people's reaction to our writing." In fact, adds Keyes, "the most common disguise is fear of *them, their* opinion of us, when it's actually our own opinion of ourselves that we're worried about." Keyes suggests that ultimately "mastering techniques [of style and craft] will do far less to improve writing than finding the will, the

251

nerve, the guts to put on paper what you really want to say."

In *The Writer's Guide to Creativity* (Writer's Digest, 1999), Keyes relates how he challenged a writing student to be more open in his prose: "Why are you scared to write what you feel?" Keyes had asked the student, who answered, "I'm not scared to write what I feel, I'm scared to *feel* what I feel." Says Keyes: "Any writing lays the writer open to judgment about the quality of his work and thought. The closer he gets to painful personal truths, the more fear mounts—not just about what he might reveal, but about what he might discover should he venture too deeply inside. *But to write well, that's exactly where we must venture.*"

So, why do it, then? Why bother? Is it worth it to make yourself totally vulnerable to the possible censure and ridicule of your peers, friends, and relatives? To serve up your heart on a platter to just have them drag it around as Stevie Nicks would say…

The Secret of Success

> If I ever go looking for my heart's desire again, I won't look any further than my own back yard. Because if it isn't there, I never really lost it to

252

begin with
—Dorothy Gale, The Wizard of OZ

Welcome to the threshold of your career as a writer. This is where many aspiring writers stop: in abject fear, not just of failure but of success. The only difference between those that don't and those that do, is that the former come to terms with their fears, in fact learn to use them as a barometer to what is important.

How do you get past the fear of being exposed, past the anticipated disappointment of peers, past the terror of success?

The answer is passion. If you are writing about something you are passionate about, you will find the courage to see it through. "The more I read, and write," says Keyes:

> *The more convinced I am that the best writing flows less from acquired skill than conviction expressed with courage. By this I don't mean moral convictions, but the sense that what one has to say is something others need to know.*

This is ultimately what drives a writer to not just write but to publish: the need to share one's story, over and over again. Some of us only have one story we need to tell (Margaret Mitchell only needed to tell one, *Gone With the Wind*); others of us have many to tell. Either way, what is key here is that to prevail, persist, and ultimately succeed, a writer must have conviction and believe in his or her writing. You must believe that you have something to say that others want to read. Ask yourself why you are a writer. Your answer might surprise you.

Every writer is an artist. And every artist is a cultural reporter. One who sometimes holds the world accountable. "Real art," says Susan Sontag, "makes us nervous."

> *Artists—we love 'em and we hate 'em. On the one hand we call them kooks: on the other hand, we look to them for our reflection. We ask them to tell us who we are. But we get nervous when their answers hit too close to home. We have a secret admiration for their irreverence, because down deep we would be irreverent too, if we weren't such 'fraidy cats. So we let them do it for us. It's easy to write them off, particularly when their hair is green*
> —Nancy Slonim Aronie

The first step, then, is to acknowledge your passion and *own* it. Flaunt it, even. Find your conviction, define what matters and explore it to the fullest. You will find that such an acknowledgement will give you the strength and fortitude to persist and persevere, particularly in the face of those fears. Use the fears to guide you into that journey of personal truths. Frederick Busch described it this way: "You go to dark places so that you can get there, steal the trophy and get out."

Every writer, like his or her protagonist, is on a

Hero's Journey (see Chapter J). Like the Hero of our epic, we too must acknowledge the call, pass the threshold guardian, experience the abyss and face the beast before we can return "home" with our prize.

This reminds me of what John Steinbeck, author of *Grapes of Wrath*, said:

> *If there is a magic in story writing, and I am convinced that there is, no one has ever been able to reduce it to a recipe that can be passed from one person to another. The formula seems to lie solely in the aching urge of the writer to convey something he feels important to the reader*
> —John Steinbeck

"Everyone is afraid to write," says Keyes. "They should be. Writing is dangerous...To love writing, fear writing and pray for the courage to write is no contradiction. It's the essence of what we do." It is the essence of what we are compelled to do. Think of it this way; what is the alternative?

Margot Finke, author of *How to Keep Your Passion and Survive as a Writer*, defines a writer's passion this way: it's "what has you up at 2 am, pounding the keys. It sneaks you into the bathroom after midnight to make notes of the terrific scene that just popped into your head. It's what puts the notebook and pen in your pocket when you go to the store—in case a great chapter idea surfaces between the broccoli aisle and the chopped beef...For the passionate, writing is not a choice; it's a force that cannot be denied."

Finding the Courage to Dream

> *I write for the same reason I breathe—because if I didn't, I would die*
> —Isaac Asimov

"If you long to excel as a writer," says Finke, "treasure the passion that is unique within yourself. Take the irreplaceable elements of your life and craft them into your own personal contribution to the world."

> *Go confidently in the direction of your dreams. Live the life you've imagined*
> —Henry David Thoreau

While passion is number one on her list of ingredients to a writer's success, Finke also includes: talent; basic writing skills; the willingness to work hard; the ability to survive rejection; knowing the publishing industry, good researching skills, and persistence, what she calls "stick-with-it-ness".

All of these tools are acquired through our love of our craft and our passion for storytelling. As artists, we are compelled to engage and share. Passion fuels our art. It fires us to persist. It gives us patience and the strength to work hard and pursue our journey.

Passion Gets You Published!

> *Look round the habitable world, how few know their own good, or, knowing it, pursue*
> —Juvenal

Finke says it astutely: You need to be passionate about everything to do with your book—the writing and rewriting, your critique group, your research, your search for the best agent/editor, plus your query letter. Not to mention the passion that goes into promoting your book. Nothing less will assure your survival—and success—as a writer.

Dreaming Big

Most writers dream of writing a bestseller although only a handful achieve this status. The irony is that the big secret of achieving bestseller stature and becoming wildly popular is not what you think it is.

You thought I was going to send you to the bookstore to research the market, weren't you? Or go to Amazon and find out what's selling? Or see who and what is currently on the bestseller list?

While these are all valid quests, writing to the market will not ensure that your work becomes a bestseller. In fact, it will likely do the opposite.

When a writer is writing to the market, she is **following** the market, not **leading** it. Here lies the rub—a book becomes a bestseller because it provides something new and refreshing to a wide readership, eager for a story that resonates with originality. This isn't necessarily something eclectic and strange; but it is most certainly a new voice and/or new way of looking at something familiar.

When a unique voice intersects with a popular thought, a bestseller emerges.

That is precisely what happened with *Harry Potter*. J.K. Rowling didn't invent wizards or fantasy or even a school for wizards; but she did provide a fresh look at the popular subject of an outsider who finds that he is special. And let's not forget that before her book became a bestseller, it was rejected many times by less visionary publishers unwilling to take a risk.

So, what am I advising? Find your own voice, the one that belongs only to you. Cultivate your unique voice and write with passion. Write about something that means a lot to you or excites you or intrigues you. Be genuine. Be specific. Put yourself out there. Take risks. And be patient. Chances are, your writing will resonate with many. But don't sweat it; enjoy the journey.

Arthur Miller, author of *Death of a Salesman*, wisely advised that you "develop interest in life as you see it; in people, things, literature, music—the world is so rich, simply throbbing with treasures, beautiful souls and interesting people. *Forget yourself.*"

The Gestalt Nature of Passion & Success

> *What is to give light must endure burning*
> —Victor Frankl

Victor Frankl survived Auschwitz to become an important neurologist and psychiatrist of our time and to write *Man's Search for Meaning*. Blogger Gavin Ortlund wrote: "What gripped me most about [Frankl's] book, and has stayed with me to this day, is not the horror and barbarity of his experiences in concentration camps—when you pick up a book about the holocaust, you expect that. What really struck me was Frankl's repeated insistence that even there, in the most inhumane and horrific conditions imaginable, the greatest struggle is not mere survival. The greatest struggle is finding meaning. As I was reading, I was struck with this thought: going to a concentration camp is not the worst thing that can happen to a person. The worst that can happen to a person is not having a transcendent reason to live. Life is about more than finding comfort and avoiding suffering: it's about finding what is ultimate, whatever the cost."

Victor Frankl said:

> *The more you aim at success and make it a target, the more you are going to miss it. ...Success, like happiness, cannot be pursued; it must ensue, and it only does so as the unintended side effect of one's personal dedication to a cause greater than oneself or as the by-*

259

product of one's surrender to a person other than oneself. Happiness must happen, and the same holds for success: you have to let it happen by not caring about it. I want you to listen to what your conscience commands you to do and go on to carry it out to the best of your knowledge. Then you will live to see that in the long-run - in the long-run, I say! - success will follow you precisely because you had forgotten to think about it.

References

Finke, Margot. 2008. "How to Keep Your Passion and Survive as a Writer." In: *The Purple Crayon*, http://www.underdown.org/mf_writing_passion

Frankl, Victor. (1946) 1997. *Man's Search for Meaning.* Pocket Books. 224 pp.

Keyes, Ralph. 1999. *The Writer's Guide to Creativity.* Writer's Digest, 1999.

Ortlund, Gavin. 2008. "Frankl, the holocaust and meaning." In: Let Us Hold Fast. http://gro1983.blogspot.com/2008/02/frankl-holocaust-and-meaning.html

Slonim Aronie, Nancy. 1998. *Writing from the Heart: Tapping the Power of Your Inner Voice.* Hyperion. 256pp.

Index:

● About the Author

Nina Munteanu is **the Passionate Writer**. She has authored several novels and award-nominated short stories. Her latest book, *Darwin's Paradox*, was nominated for the *Aurora Prix*, Canada's top prize in science fiction. Nina is an ecologist and teaches university courses in science and environmental education. She regularly speaks at writers' conferences and gives workshops based on this modular course. Nina is a contributing author of Suite 101, and served as assistant editor-in-chief of *Imagikon*, Romania's speculative ezine. Nina regularly publishes critical reviews and essays in magazines, among them *The New York Review of Science Fiction* and *Strange Horizons*. Her award-winning blog, *The Alien Next Door*, hosts lively discussion on science, pop culture, writing and philosophy. To book Nina's online classes visit www.thepassionatewriter.com.

Acknowledgements

I borrowed from the wisdom of many authorities on the subject of writing and publishing, notably Robert J. Sawyer, Elizabeth Lyon, Ansen Dibell, Crawford Killian, Elsa Neal, Sol Stein, Margot Finke, Jack Bickham, Janet Fitch and Marg Gilks, Any mistakes are mine, not theirs. Special thanks go to Virginia O'Dine for cover art and typography. I am greatly indebted to Clélie Rich for her impeccable proofreading. Thanks also go to Anne Voûte for comments on the manuscript and to Teresa Young for lively and erudite discussions on writing and philosophy. I give my heart-felt thanks to Karen Mason, of *Starfire World Syndicate*, for mentoring in matters technical and editorial but mostly for making dreams come true.

264